The Digital Marketing Landscape

The Digital Marketing Landscape

Creating a Synergistic Consumer Experience

Jessica L. Rogers

Leader in applied, concise business books

The Digital Marketing Landscape: Creating a Synergistic Consumer Experience

Copyright © Business Expert Press, LLC, 2021.

Cover design by Charlene Kronstedt

Interior design by Exeter Premedia Services Private Ltd., Chennai, India

First published in 2021 by
Business Expert Press, LLC
222 East 46th Street, New York, NY 10017
www.businessexpertpress.com

ISBN-13: 978-1-63742-034-8 (paperback)
ISBN-13: 978-1-63742-035-5 (e-book)

Business Expert Press Digital and Social Media Marketing and Advertising Collection

Collection ISSN: 2333-8822 (print)
Collection ISSN: 2333-8830 (electronic)

First edition: 2021

10 9 8 7 6 5 4 3 2 1

Description

The field of marketing has seen an evolution in how brands communicate with consumers, how consumers communicate with brands, and how consumers communicate with one another. Digital technologies such as mobile phones, the internet, social media, and email contribute to what is known as the digital marketing landscape. Digital marketing offers unique ways to meet consumers where they are, engage with potential and existing consumers, capture the voice of the consumer; allow consumers to be part of a brand narrative.

This book is geared towards both students and professionals looking to explore the interconnectedness of digital technologies for marketing and branding purposes. This book offers an overview of the digital marketing landscape and how the various elements of digital can work synergistically. When the power of an integrated digital strategy is optimized, both consumers and brands benefit.

The Digital Marketing Landscape serves as a practical guide for both students and professionals in a variety of settings. Readers will become familiar with terminology, understand how the different areas of digital marketing connect and work together, and gain the knowledge needed to generate valuable and actionable managerial insights for more informed decision-making.

Keywords

digital marketing; social media marketing; SEO; SEM; PPC; e-mail marketing; content marketing; branding; blogging; online experience

Contents

Reviewers

"A brand is nothing but a promise delivered. Marketing has evolved dramatically, becoming even more present in the digital age. Dr. Jessica Rogers's book serves as the perfect guide for anyone looking to understand the intricacies of branding, marketing, and how each brand delivers on their promises to their customers." —**Jeffrey Hayzlett, Primetime TV & Podcast Host, Speaker, Author and Part-Time Cowboy**

"It's never been more essential, and more difficult, to create a delightful, integrated, end-to-end experience for your customer and consumers of your brand. Dr. Rogers's book, 'The Digital Marketing Landscape', is a welcome and lucid manual to accomplishing that critical goal. This book is an important and critical reading for those who realize that how you sell/market is just as important as what you sell/market." —**Isaac Moche, Senior Manager of Academy Programs, HubSpot**

"Rogers has provided a compelling 31,000-foot view of marketing in the digital age. As an educator in this area, she is constantly exposed to new ideas and has a responsibility of sharing these ideas with her students, as is clearly demonstrated in this book. She has several key takeaways that resonated with me, to include:

- *The idea of "digital marketing" has evolved over time and has now become an umbrella term to describe the process of using digital technologies to acquire customers and build customer preferences, promote brands, retain customers, and increase sales.*
- *A good marketer knows who their target customers are inside and out.*
- *The combination of being a marketing expert who also encompass some technical skills associated with digital will become a prerequisite for employment within the field.*

These are just a few of the many "nuggets" in this book. It is a quick read that is definitely worth your time." —**Jeff Sheehan, Thought Leader, Sheehan Marketing Strategies**

"This is a perfect book for anyone who wants to improve their understanding of digital media, email and SEO to apply to a business. Learn how to harness the power of technology and social media to solve problems and reach your goals." —**Dr. Nancy Richmond, Professor & Consultant**

"Too many businesses take a scattered approach to digital marketing and don't leverage the available opportunities. "The Digital Marketing Landscape: Creating a Synergistic Consumer Experience" takes the reader through a comprehensive and synergistic plan to cut through the noise and get results. In a world of shiny object syndrome, this book puts all the puzzle pieces into place and ensures you are focusing on the right things. A worthwhile read!" —**Melonie Dodaro, Author of LinkedIn Unlocked**

"The Digital Marketing Landscape is an accessible while advancing text. You'll get the macro landscape of marketing, but also get tangible ways to apply to specific platforms and tools. I loved how Dr. Rogers approached creating a synergistic consumer experience through the grounding of human connection, authentic content, and truly knowing your community." —**Dr. Josie Ahlquist, Digital Leadership Author, Consultant, and Speaker**

"In this ground-breaking book, Dr. Jessica Rogers deftly presents various frameworks that help the reader better understand how digital technologies will continue to underpin successful marketing and branding strategies over the next decade. The Digital Marketing Landscape should be on every marketer's desk, from the Fortune 500 CMO to the aspiring intern." —**Kent Huffman, CEO & Fractional CMO, DigiMark Partners**

"Your brand's digital footprint may be more important than your logo, and it changes daily. All of the digital pieces of a marketing effort must work together to advance a brand and customer awareness. Whether you call it the "digital marketing landscape," "D-Marketingscape," or "D-IMC," Dr. Rogers has provided a practical guide to orchestrating the digital efforts of a company and

brand. This book is an actionable resource for brand managers, marketers, growth hackers, and students of marketing…" —**Gary R. Schirr, Associate Professor, Radford University**

"A must read for anyone in marketing." —**Steve Olenski, The CMO Whisperer**

"Rogers has created a practical roadmap for today's marketing challenges. Driven by a focus on marketing's role as architect of an experience, this book plots the intersections between digital communication assets and the creation of awareness and brand equity in the marketplace. But unlike discussions preoccupied with one-off viral moments, this is a volume for everyone aspiring to create an aligned strategy that delivers lasting value, thereby inspiring action and loyalty." —**Eric R. Fletcher, Founder/CEO, Eric Fletcher Consulting**

"Dr. Jessica Rogers distills the essential knowledge, skills, and abilities for the modern marketer to create robust relationships with their audience, through digital avenues. This book is a useful tool for learners as well as marketing practitioners and business owners of all sizes looking to build their brand." —**Dr. Cali Morrison, Certified Professional Coach, Founder, Creative Synapse, LLC and Interim Dean, Center for Professional & Continuing Education, American Public University System**

"In The Digital Marketing Landscape, Rogers integrates digital modes and technologies to demonstrate to readers how these modes can operate synergistically. As a practical guide, the book offers much needed advice and prescriptions for students and marketing professionals alike." —**Dr. Tracy Tuten, Author of Social Media Marketing**

Introduction

As we go through our day-to-day lives, both professional and personal, it is imperative to always be learning, and to always be improving so we can be our best selves. In my role as an educator, I am able to see first-hand how learning is not only essential for continued growth and fulfillment, but it also provides learners with a sense of ownership over their own journey. Learning can also, in many cases, change the trajectory of one's life and impact future generations.

It is my hope that this book will provide some direction to the reader, likely business professionals seeking to digest the main components of the digital landscape to better understand the intersection of the various platforms, and to be better able to communicate with those who work within the digital landscape. Or, a future business leader exploring the facets of digital marketing, with hopes of discovering a passion and potential career path. Regardless of what prompted you to pick up this book, this brief read will provide you with a crash course on the various platforms and tools digital marketers should be familiar with. As you read, pay particular attention to how the elements can work together. Think about yourself as a consumer, and how an integrated and strategic approach may influence your purchase decisions and overall consumer behaviors. Each chapter offers a few learning objectives to guide your thoughts as you reflect on the readings. At the end of the text, you will find additional information surrounding associated certifications that will further support your learning and add to your employability.

The American Marketing Association defines marketing as "the activity, set of institutions, and processes for creating, communicating, delivering, and exchanging offerings that have value for customers, clients, partners, and society at large (American Marketing Association 2020). So therefore, it stands to reason the idea of focusing on the value creation in our digital efforts is a key component of marketing efforts. Through the strategic process of creating content and sharing content as marketers via digital platforms, we are creating relevance and value. Although this may come in a variety of forms, the focus on the creation of value is paramount. As you read about the various digital platforms, players, and tools, how can you create value for your customers? What do your customers deem as valuable?

I hope to inspire you to embark on your own digital exploration and begin to utilize digital more fully to tell your brand's story, while also allowing the consumer to contribute to the narrative. It is my hope that this text will spark new and innovative ideas on how you can utilize digital tools more effectively if you are already involved in some form of digital marketing, or to use digital in new and innovative ways within your industry.

CHAPTER 1

The Digital Brand Experience

Learning Objectives

- Understand how organizations promote brand awareness and differentiation through current digital technologies.
- Understand strategic marketing approaches for optimizing exposure of brand narratives across digital platforms.
- Explore the idea of Inbound Marketing and how digital supports this method.

The field of marketing has seen an evolution in how brands communicate with consumers, how consumers communicate with brands, and how consumers communicate with one another. Digital technologies such as mobile phones, the Internet, social media, and e-mail contribute to what is known as the digital marketing landscape. The digital landscape goes above and beyond what the traditional forms of communication such as print, radio, and TV are able to contribute to building brands and impacting interest (Kannan and Li 2017). Digital offers the ability to reach customers to promote products and services, while also providing significant value to customers, and contribute to branding efforts. Digital marketing has evolved, and the associated digital technologies are creating value in new ways through new customer experiences, through new types of interactions, and through a series of new adaptive touch points (Kannan and Li 2017). Given its unique ability to engage consumers and communities, digital can be a very powerful tool for not only building brands, but strengthening relationships as well (Aaker 2015). Digital is no longer future state; it is here and now. A well-crafted digital marketing strategy will help an organization build a strong online reputation, increase brand awareness, encourage traffic, and lead to conversions that will result in increased customers, sales, growth, and success (Ahuja and Loura 2018).

When you think about the components of the digital marketing landscape, consider your daily interactions with the many marketing messages from the perspective of a consumer. For example, you are in the market for a pair of new running shoes. Your first inclination may be to Google "running shoes for high arches." This search will result in several suggested articles, advertisements, or other content ranging from branded material to unbranded material from this search. You may then read several articles associated with the search, be pulled toward retailer sites, or even be exposed to information that will alter your initial search. The typical consumer will read reviews on retailer websites, read blog posts and other articles related to the purchasing decision, ask friends via social media, and they may even be doing this all from a mobile device. Should the consumer be performing these searches and research via mobile device, there's also the opportunity to simply complete the process and make a purchase with a click of a button.

In this very rudimentary example, the components of the digital marketing landscape create an "experience" for the consumer. All of these elements (websites, images, social media content, mobile application content, and more) should portray the same brand image in the consumers' mind and convey the same marketing messages, while also contributing to overall branding efforts. Imagine the various elements of digital marketing technologies as a piece of a puzzle. Each piece fits with other pieces (hopefully seamlessly) to result in a cohesive picture.

While the basic principles of marketing have remained the same, the ways in which we accomplish marketing goals have seen significant advancements in recent years. Among the many challenges for marketers today is the creation and retention of loyal customer groups (Aaker and Marcum 2017). The digital landscape of today adds many complexities to brand building such as ever-changing media, on-demand expectations, consumers now having more control, the difficulties associated with effective integration of messages, and the subsequent impact on delivering on brand customer experiences. Marketers must also compete with more "noise" than ever before to reach consumers. The consumer of today has a much shorter attention span than in the past and many have embraced an "on-demand" mentality. Digital marketing offers unique ways to meet consumers where they are and to break through the "noise." Digital allows brands to engage with potential and existing consumers and to capture the voice of the consumer, all the while allowing consumers to be part of a brand's marketing message and narrative. New and innovative technologies are allowing marketers to target specific audiences with personalized digital content that contributes to the development of consumer awareness, facilitate sales, and impacts trust and loyalty. Content that is informative, entertaining, functional, and resonates with the audience is a backbone for a strategic approach.

One of the most valuable assets an organization has is the brand names associated with their products or services (Keller 2013). The key to effective branding is for consumers to perceive differences between brands in a particular category; utilizing digital allows marketers to make those differences more recognizable through a strategic narrative. Digital marketing, and the associated digital brand engagement, involves a disciplined and strategic approach to ensure more meaningful and intimate connections. Just as a logo is considered part of a brand, a brand's digital footprint is as well. From a company webpage, to its social media profiles, to its e-mail content, and mobile applications, it all represents a brand and contributes to a narrative surrounding that brand. The notion of a "brand" via a marketing lens is important as it helps to achieve a competitive advantage (Kapferer 2004). If leveraged appropriately, all of these assets help to create meaningful connections and opportunities to engage with consumers. The development of a strong brand identity over several digital channels is considered digital branding (Poulis et al. 2017). Digital channels offer much more flexibility in terms of the length of content, costs, and availability as opposed to traditional media such as magazines or television. As we proceed through this book, think about how the platforms and tools can be used to create and broadcast this narrative. Reflect on the narratives you consume each day in your personal and professional lives. How do these narratives impact your behavior as a consumer?

Brand awareness relates to brand recognition and brand recall (Keller 2013), and it plays an important role in the consumer decision-making process. When a consumer is confronted with multiple brands, will they be able to recognize a brand as one they have previously been exposed to; will they recall a brand from memory when thinking of a specific brand category? Consider how these elements impact a purchase decision, and how digital can help with brand awareness via social media posts, digital advertisements, e-mail communications, and other digital platforms. Once an organization has established a sufficient level of awareness for the brand, the next step is creating a brand's image. The brand image reflects the perceptions consumers may have of the brand. Brand awareness and positing brand image directly correlates to brand equity. And to build brand equity, you must shape how consumers think and feel about your product (Keller 2013).

An organization's website may detail offerings and host additional content to contribute to brand image, while their social profiles share similar content, but also allow for engagement with their audience. Similarly, the organization's e-mail database offers a direct path to a consumer to pull them along through the decision-making and purchase-making process, while an associated branded mobile application facilitates the purchase process or engagement with the brand. An organization may have an excellent product or service, but in what ways are they able to communicate this with consumers and potential customers while also facilitating engagement with the company? Marketers have many more tools in their toolbelt than just a decade ago. The idea of branding is not new, but it has become an actionable buzzword in the marketing landscape as we see new digital technologies abound that are breathing new life to almost extinct brands.

Digital marketing does not solely revolve around digital tools and data. Effective digital marketers understand the relationship between the various digital platforms and associated tools, and the intersection with an organization's overall marketing strategy. Further, they understand the relationship between the brand and the consumer and how to best engage digitally in a meaningful, personalized, and relevant manner. They understand customers are connected and informed, as well as empowered. And, they understand digital marketing contributes to the future of a brand and the customer experience. The creation of an excellent digital experience takes into account all facets of digital marketing as one cohesive unit.

When considering a strategy for digital, one must begin with goals. As we know, goals should speak to an organization's defined mission and vision. These goals will inform each area of your strategic approach to digital. These goals will also scaffold to the tactics you choose to use via digital technologies, and ultimately how you will measure success. When formulating a digital strategy, it is paramount to be extremely specific with setting goals as you begin to strategize. As you try to determine the goals of your strategy, think about how your efforts might tie to rebranding or branding, promoting brand awareness, differentiating your product or service from the competition, communicating value propositions, impacting consumer sentiment, promoting your organization's unique selling proposition, and more. As goals become more clearly defined, one is better able to see how each of the digital technologies will contribute.

In the past, we relied on the one-to-many approach; we had to push our messages to mass audiences with little differentiation in content or target audience. The message from brand to consumer is then perceived by the consumer as advertising, and thus less meaningful. In today's digital environment, we are able to provide a much richer experience for both the consumer and the organization. Marketers are able to contribute to brand building by essentially giving a brand a digital personality and making sustained connections with consumers through digital channels. Through a variety of consumer experiences or marketing activities, many brands take on personality traits or values. Digital channels allow a brand to exhibit human-like characteristics like humor, authority, fun-loving, trustworthy, warm, or even glamorous.

Customers often interact with brands as though they are real live people (Aaker 1996), and we see this play out on social media in particular. It is not uncommon for brands to embrace their unique personalities within their Tweets on Twitter; it has even become a trend for brands to do this with one another using catchy hashtags and GIFs. A brand may choose to create this image and personality via digital technologies such as social media posts, viral videos, visuals on websites and in e-mails, and more. It is worth noting that once a personality has been established, it becomes very difficult for a consumer to accept anything that is incongruent to that personality. Consumers tend to choose brands that have a brand personality that is consistent or much like their own self-concept.

They may relate to the image and reputation of a brand that defines their perceived unique behavioral characteristics. However, some consumers may align with a brand based on their own desired image as opposed to their actual image. Consumers may find it aspirational to be identified with brand signs and symbols; there can be symbolic associations for the consumer.

Consumers and brands today now have many touch points, and thus, many opportunities to ensure a consolidated "branded" message. However, it is important to understand that the notion of branding is not simply the logo, the product, or the service. It is much more than that; it also encompasses customer service, employees, brand-generated content and user-generated content, engagement via digital channels, and more. Simply having more touch points does not equate to increased influence (Kotler et al. 2017). Brands need to push to differentiate themselves in meaningful ways, connect with customers in ways that add value, and focus efforts on leveraging the power of digital connectivity to strengthen relationships. Marketers need to drive initiatives across an organization to ensure a brand delivers on its promises everywhere along the consumer journey.

Brand strategies help to establish a clear and distinctive identity for your products, services, and the organization overall (Romo et al. 2017). The importance of building your brand internally cannot be understated. When employees know the reason a brand exists, and the mission and vision behind strategic initiatives, they will find a higher sense of purpose. Internal branding impacts everyone from the frontline employee who deals directly with the consumer, to those working in nonconsumer-facing roles. This is especially important for service-oriented firms such as Southwest Airlines and specialty retailers like Nordstrom. The consistent external branding messages must also be consistent internally. Employees who "get it" will be imperative to all digital initiatives from user experience design, to content creation, to content curation, to those who engage via social on behalf of the brand, and all the way to the employee who may be interacting with consumers offline in a brick and mortar facility.

Branding is based on making human and emotional connections. Our consumer of today in this digital environment demands that connection and personal attention. In order for a brand to thrive, the brand must work to create an emotional connection with customers that cannot be easily replicated. Brands that are able to foster a sense of community and resonate with the consumer will be able to sustain disruptive and turbulent times. The importance of achieving that emotional connection cannot be understated. Marketers must strive to develop and uplift brands in order to secure emotional investment along with market share. Strong brands are critical financial assets that will contribute to sustainable growth over time.

It has never been more important for a brand to authentically communicate who they are, what they stand for, what they do, and how the consumer perceives them, than ever before. A brand is built through brand attitude, brand attachment, brand involvement, brand personality, customer delight, and brand experience (Brakus et al. 2009). The brand experience in the digital age should be one that helps create a connected and customer-obsessed experience. Brands that are able to distinguish themselves among consumers will have a leg up, and how they choose to do this impacts all points of strategic digital marketing. In a time where consumers have so many options for purchases, effective branding and brand building in a very strategic and integrated way will differentiate the winners from losers.

Customers, Target Audiences, and Buyer Personas

Customers today expect a certain level of authenticity and relevancy and have somewhat higher expectations. As marketers, we are charged with meeting their needs and expectations at the right time with the right offer, via the right channel. The idea of throwing out many approaches and seeing what "sticks" (like cooking pasta) is by no means effective or sustainable. Here is where the idea of a target market or target audience comes in to play. A target market, or more specifically, a target audience, describes a particular audience of consumers who will find your product or service the most relevant. The term target audience is generally more popular among business to consumer (B2C) companies than business to business (B2B). The identification of a target market or audience will allow you to tailor your strategy to fit the target. Targeting is a fundamental aspect of a brand strategy (Kotler et al. 2017). However, there are still companies who feel that everyone, or everyone who buys their product or service, is a target. This could not be further from the truth. This view is held by those who presume if you market to all, all will buy. Instead, ask yourself who is the end user, and who is *not* the end user.

Understanding consumers is fundamental to traditional marketing; it is also fundamental to digital marketing. A good marketer knows who their target customers are inside and out. As we look to the online or digital customer, this becomes even more important, given the geographic barriers are less confining and attitudes in online shopping differ than brick and mortar. Interestingly, a consumer may actually behave differently in the digital space as a consumer than they do in the traditional offline landscape. A solid understanding is absolutely paramount in order to craft an effective strategy regardless of the product, service, marketing channel you may utilize and more. The creation of profiles that identify the needs of the consumer allows for a much more strategic approach to marketing efforts. Also important in this work is the identification of problems your target audience may have that your company can solve. This work can then be translated to multiple channels with the digital landscape.

When planning a strategic approach to digital marketing, along with setting goals and exploring target audiences, consider: Who do we want to show our marketing messages to? What technologies do they use? Does it make more sense to send marketing messages out via Twitter? Or does it make more sense to utilize e-mail marketing? The identification of a target audience will impact nearly every facet of your strategy. It will impact the images you use, the content you share, the platform you choose to share it on, the keywords you utilize, and the tools you leverage throughout implementation. Through digital, marketers are able to increase their reach by exposing advertisements and/or content to a new audience, or reinforce brand messages with the use of a current and defined segment (Poulis et al. 2017). This highly defined target becomes easy to identify through effective use of data that comes from a variety of sources such as web history, social media postings, and user profiles.

Also important in this planning stage is the idea of buyer personas. Buyer personas are somewhat fictional character representations of your preferred user or buyer based on marketing research and what you know about your existing customer. Notice the difference between a buyer persona and a target audience. Your target audience may be a group of the population you wish to target your marketing messages to. However, a buyer persona offers significantly more detail; it allows you a more insightful look at motivations and goals. A buyer persona is used more often by the B2B segment and is considered a subset of an ideal customer profile. Identifying and defining the types of people who will be most receptive to your product or service (or solution to their problem) is the first step to an effective buyer persona.

The process of creating a buyer persona is much like target audience identification: you will explore demographic, psychographic, and behavioral information. But with buyer persona, you will go a bit further to explore goals and motivations as well. The notion of creating and utilizing a persona embodies a consumer-centered approach. Personas were initially created by Cooper (1999) as a way to create a hypothetical user. Personas are able to provide a means for capturing both qualitative and quantitative data in an easy to digest manner; however, some believe creating personas leads to stereotypes (Turner and Turner 2011). It is very common for marketers to utilize a buyer persona when strategizing and brainstorming about marketing messages. We want these messages to resonate and evoke action. In order to do this, we need to know about the buyer on a much deeper level.

Buyer personas are often a product of research, surveys, and interviews of multiple types of people. You may research a mix of customers, prospects, and even others outside of your contacts database who might align with your target audience. It is not uncommon to create a character based on these personas with a fictitious name and image. These images or characters are used by marketers to create a more intimate relationship by being able to envision who these persons are and what motivates them. The creation and utilization of personas in marketing embodies a user-centric approach. Having a deep understanding of your buyer personas will help in your planning for just about anything related to customer acquisition and retention. The customer persona, in general, informs the customer journey map. This customer journey is a sequence of points where a consumer has direct or indirect touch points with a product brand or service. The customer experience at each of these touch points impacts the perceived relationship quality between brand and consumer. Keep in mind that these touch points may occur offline and online, and this journey is structured sequentially. Once armed with a buyer persona, it becomes much easier to determine the best course of action for creating and disseminating marketing messages as part of a digital strategy or campaign.

Inbound Marketing

The idea of sending one-to-many communications is no longer as effective as it once was. Organizations need to promote themselves through digital technologies to bring customers to the brand. Marketers must look to pull the consumer to the brand and guide them through the customer journey in a one-on-one scenario. Thus, it is important to understand what the customer journey looks like from the consumer point of view. A customer journey map is imperative as it will provide data to inform decision making. Both the consumer and the brand must actively participate in this process to make meaningful connections and create experiences that are valuable for both parties. These connections contribute to the customer experience and build upon branding initiatives. Digital mediums offer marketers a measurable way to strategically initiate connections with prospective consumers. Digital also allows for personalization, building trust and relationships, facilitating real-time engagement, and impacting customer retention and associated strategies. All of these elements contribute to the digital brand experience.

Nearly every business will strategically focus on the idea of generating leads, making sales, capturing new customers, and retaining the consumers they already have. Upon delving deeper, such goals require different approaches. As a marketer, you must decide what you want your digital marketing campaign to accomplish. This all stems from first identifying business objectives as these objectives will speak directly to the type of campaign employed and the tactics used within the campaign. One reason many new businesses do not achieve the success they had hoped relates back to not having objectives clearly agreed upon and the business just diving into digital tools (such as building a website or starting a social media feed) without having determined objectives and strategy first. It is like building a home without a blueprint. Having a clear picture of business objectives will make setting goals and defining a digital marketing campaign significantly more effective (Chaffey and Smith 2017). Some businesses choose a strategy that will help build brand community, or inform and acquire new leads and customers, monetize leads and customers to generate revenue, or even increase brand awareness. Worth noting, one approach does not trump the others. A successful brand will strive to run a combination of campaigns. Running a campaign to acquire new customers does not necessarily have the same outcome as a campaign to build community or a campaign to monetize existing customers. For example, the notion of blogging is phenomenal for growing brand awareness and providing informational content to prospective consumers. However, there is a little chance, if any, to monetize.

The traditional notion of a campaign assumes a specified start and end date. However, a digital campaign could run from as short as one day (think prepping and promoting a flash sale on Instagram or the like) to several years. In a traditional marketing setting, a campaign may be several weeks of direct marketing to consumers for a specific goal and objective. Once deployed, it becomes difficult to tweak the approach. A digital campaign allows marketers to be significantly more agile, enabling us to make minor tweaks and to optimize a digital marketing strategy as needed.

Crafting, curating, and generating relevant content through every stage of the customer journey will impact customer satisfaction and opportunities for the brand to engage with the consumer. Not to mention the increase in conversions from lead to customer, and brand loyalty to boot! Loyalty is considered to be the strength of the relationship between an individual's relative attitude and repeat patronage (Dick and Basu 1994). Failure to utilize content that your audience deems valuable or helpful will lead to less than stellar results. If you are not providing content that resonates and engages the audience, you will be unable to create and nurture meaningful relationships. Content can be created or curated and can come in many forms. Video is hugely popular, along with other visuals like GIFs, infographics, and podcasts. This content contributes to your brand and brand personality (and thus authenticity) and can also be used as an inbound approach, pulling the consumer toward you via the content that is shared on multiple channels. Curation of content from other sources can be a good way to show your audience it is not all about you. It shows you are engaging about all things that resonate with your audience but do be sure you are sharing credible content from credible sources, and giving credit where credit is due. Curating content is also a good way to fill up your content calendar when you may not have enough original created content to fill it, or if you are seeking something specific that is not your area of expertise, or even to simply show you keep up with the current news and industry trends. This is yet one more way to differentiate your brand from the competition.

Regardless of the technological advances, marketing is still focused on a mutually beneficial relationship between customers and brands. The development of this relationship can be tied to the customer journey. Consider the example earlier, searching for new running shoes. Digital marketing helps us in moving a potential lead from one stage of the journey to the next. It is this journey, which may start and stop in varying places for varying consumers, that has the potential to create differentiated experiences. As a digital marketer, your job is to look at this journey and identify where you can infuse excellence via digital technologies to create an amazing customer experience. All of the research a consumer will do before purchase, the actual purchase process, and post purchase evaluation are all part of a branding narrative. Consumers see images on TV related to the product and images online via websites, blogs, and social media that influence the decision-making process, as well as consumer reviews and articles related to the product. All of these elements tie together to contribute to a brand narrative, both brand produced and consumer produced. Anyone on digital media has the ability to initiate sharing their views, feelings, and issues about a brand and associated brand experiences (Aaker 2015). Marketers will need to lead the convergence of brand and customer experiences, and marketing to deliver consistent experience across all touch points.

Think of iconic brands or brands that you associate positively with. What messages do they send you? What images do you see when you think of these brands? Now think of a brand that you may have a negative feeling about. What images do you see? What narrative do you think of?

Did this narrative come to you via brand messaging pushed toward you? Do they originate from the brand or users? Perhaps marketing messages from the brand do not resonate with you or are contradictory to your beliefs. Or, did this narrative come to you via other consumers? Perhaps you saw many negative reviews on Amazon or negative comments on Facebook about a particular brand or product. This content online is generated from both the brand and consumers.

Key Takeaways

For any type of business, this always-changing landscape can become overwhelming. The online space is very competitive, and organizations must develop their own unique marketing strategy via digital tools. The idea of "digital marketing" has evolved over time and has now become an umbrella term to describe the process of using digital technologies to acquire customers and build customer preferences, promote brands, retain customers, and increase sales (Ahuja and Loura 2018). Digital technologies facilitate the creation of marketing messages and aid in creating and delivering value for consumers through customer experience and through delivering value to other stakeholders. Digital technologies are filling gaps between customers and brands in significant ways, such as customer experiences and interactions. Digital is a critical component to branding in a competitive environment and provides marketers with new channels for customer communications and promotions (such as websites, social media, search engines, mobile, and e-mail) that can provide significant value to customers as well as acquire the right customers.

The creation and sharing of content to achieve set goals is a backbone to the coming chapters of this book, as well as a digital marketing campaign. Content serves as the foundation for your campaign and directly impacts all areas of digital marketing. From branded websites or blogs, e-mail, and social media platforms, to nonbranded content created and promoted by end users (known as user-generated content or consumer-generated content), it is all part of the narrative. You will see the idea of content marketing interwoven throughout the chapters of the book.

As you read the following chapter, understand that a digital marketing campaign varies in length depending on business goal and objectives.

It can be a continuous process, or a short campaign, and is made up of several platforms and tools used in a very strategic and cohesive manner. At the heart of any successful campaign is the alignment of business goals and objectives with your digital marketing goals, objectives, and tactics. Organizations can promote brand awareness and differentiation through a variety of technologies, but the basic tenets of marketing still apply, as does the notion of conveying your value proposition consistently online and offline. This online communication of your value proposition should reinforce core brand values and clearly outline what a customer can get from your brand that they cannot from any other brand. Tools such as social media platforms, e-mail, SEO, SEM, websites, mobile technologies, and a host of other digital tools allow an organization to optimize the exposure of brand narratives across digital platforms.

CHAPTER 2

A Framework for Search

Learning Objectives

- Explain search engine optimization and search engine marketing features
- Understand search engine strategies for promoting positive brand awareness
- Analyze strategic use of websites as part of an integrated digital strategy
- Compare how brands add value and translate customer needs into an excellent online experience

Search engines have become the most popular platforms for consumers across the globe to go to for information gathering; they are recognized as paramount to the decision-making process of consumers. Search engines allow consumers to acquire free information on products and services, as well as identify businesses that fit their search criteria (Kannan and Li 2017). Search engines like Google, Bing, and Yahoo provide both organic listings as well as paid listings in response to the key words typed into the query. Thus, we have seen the increase in popular advertising formats to include both search engine marketing (SEM), a paid strategy, and search engine optimization (SEO), an organic strategy. Think of our shoe shopping endeavor in Chapter 1. We started with a simple query on a search engine that a typical consumer might engage in. Results fall into two categories, paid and organic, SEM and SEO. The consumer is presented with search engine results that favor brands who optimized their digital assets appropriately. However, optimizing a site for such results is a lengthy and ongoing process.

The idea of the search engine being the starting point for one's journey on the Internet is commonplace. SEO, or search engine optimization, is the process of refining your website using both on-page and off-page practices to impact indexing and ranking by search engines (Dodson 2016).

In other words, SEO ensures you are using the right words to be found by your customer via Google or the like, and will likely lead to being listed on page one of search engine results. SEM involves primarily keyword-based searches. Visibility of websites on a search engine had previously been a term used by marketers to refer to both organic search activities and paid, but now is almost exclusively used to describe paid search advertising. The more visible you are on a search engine, the more brand equity and visibility you will have for your organization.

Approximately 90 percent of consumers rely on search engines, and of that number, 70 percent of those consumers become organic traffic, they are not considered paid (Poulis et al. 2017). With these kinds of numbers, every business needs to be concerned with SEO and working diligently to be on page one of search results. Keywords play a lead role in how consumers are able to find your business online, and thus, how you are able to lead in search results. Customizing your content and keywords to what an existing or potential consumer will likely be searching, will garner real results. It is also important to include updating your digital content (and associated keywords) regularly to ensure timeliness and relevancy. Keep in mind, search is not only limited to the mainstream search engines, consider social media sites and online retailers like Amazon also have search functions.

There are several forms of media that make up the overall digital experience for consumers. Paid media refers to the assets that are paid for and can increase the visibility of the brand such as a Facebook ad, display advertising, or search engine marketing. Paid or bought media are media where there is some investment to pay for site visitors, reach, or conversions through search, display ad networks, or some affiliate marketing (Chaffey and Smith 2017). Owned media refers to media that an organization has control over and maintains, such as a website, blog, or social profiles. Earned media is considered "free" promotional content that is generated, or earned, via word of mouth or word of mouse, to include social media (Poulis et al. 2017).

The idea of paid traffic contrasts organic, and is typically seen in the form of digital ads that promote your branded content on various platforms such as search engines and social media. A search engine user will notice advertising in the side bar of a typical Google search. Paid traffic may be a pay per click advertising using Google Ads, a banner ad, or even a paid advertisement on Facebook. Paid traffic is extremely powerful as it builds brands, builds awareness, and generates leads. Most of us have seen paid advertisements on Facebook or other social networks that provide targeting options for the user to target a specific audience in a geographical location. The major social media platforms (Facebook, Twitter, LinkedIn, Pinterest, Instagram, and YouTube) provide an extremely effective platform for reaching many markets.

Pay per click (PPC) is a revenue model where the advertiser pays only when a user clicks an ad (Dodson 2016). Google Ads is the most popular PPC advertising system, it enables businesses to create ads that will appear within Google's search engine and other assets. Paid search is often referred to as search engine marketing (SEM). Some marketers refer to SEM to include both SEO and PPC. PPC is highly targeted, a relevant ad with link is only displayed when a certain keyword combination is entered in the search query. There is limited wastage compared to other methods. PPC also offers digital marketers a far more reliable tracking system as ROI for specific keywords can be calculated. PPC also lends itself as a fantastic tool for remarketing and branding as well. PPC is also viewed as technically a bit easier to accomplish than SEO that requires a more sophisticated system of page optimization and link building. PPC is predictable as you are paying per click, and the process is somewhat straightforward in that positions are based on a combination of bid amount and Quality Score. PPC may not be an option for everyone. It is quite competitive and expensive, and not to mention time consuming. Often brands will find success in leveraging multiple tools and techniques and adjust as appropriate. PPC can be a great option for those in very competitive markets.

SEO involves achieving the highest ranking in an organic listing on search engines after a specific combination of keywords or phrases is entered. Your goal is to have your owned digital assets populate on page one of the search engine results. In search engines like Google, these organic listings are below the Pay Per Click (PPC). The SEO process involves setting goals, on-page optimization, off-page optimization, and analyzing. Goals, as in any situation, guide the process to specific results. On-page optimization relates to the very technical optimization of the elements of a website, think of all the items that a search engine might "crawl" and index. Off-page optimization are such techniques that are used to influence website position in organic search results. Meaning, all of the elements that give a site credibility and authority that are not managed on the site. Finally, analyzing involves reviewing the data associated with the site and determining if and what adjustments should be made to better reach the set goals, or even possibly adjusting the goals themselves.

Search engine queries result in branded and nonbranded results. Meaning, it is possible for a consumer's social media post, an online review, or even a news article to be a result of a search. This is considered earned media. Not all the results will be directly tied to your digital initiatives. This is yet another reason it is imperative to be paying attention to what is being said about your brand in the digital landscape. Monitoring the conversation surrounding your brand will be a key initiative to contribute to the narrative and to engage with consumers and potential consumers as well. There may be cases where false information is shared, or your brand is being attacked, in these instances a brand should be in the position to respond, or at least know about the conversations happening online about the issue. Many brands, such as Southwest Airlines, have command centers where they monitor the discussion's happening online surrounding their brand, and they engage! Think of the digital landscape as a cocktail party, a brand must be involved and engaged with the folks at the party, as opposed to sitting out as a wallflower, or worse, sitting at home instead.

SEO is an extremely cost-effective way to increase site traffic and rank higher on search engine results pages. Search engine results page (SERP), can be a page like Google or another search engine that returns a list of "findings" in result to a query. An SERP will have results at the top, that are "paid" listings, then "organic" search results. Your goal should always be to have the first organic result in search. It is very likely a consumer will not look to page two of results, and will value the first page as more authoritative, and thus, those links will receive more clicks, and will ultimately impact your conversion rates. Conversion rate is the rate at which a visitor to your site completes a transaction or goal (Dodson 2016), such as subscribing to a newsletter or clicking to "learn more." This is made possible by driving consumers to your site, so it becomes imperative to strive to have first page ranking in search engine results pages (SERP).

The Optimized Website

A branded website is a central node for the digital landscape, explaining and enhancing other platforms and associated content. Usability, accessibility, and persuasion should be at the forefront of a web strategy and design, with attention to full integration with other marketing activities. An effective website will be able to clearly explain and enhance almost all brand building initiatives, and becomes a part of the offering by enhancing the value proposition and the perceptions of consumers. By optimizing your website through SEO, you are more likely to rank well in search results.

Your site should be adaptive to any device, tablet, mobile, and desktop. Simply designing a website for desktop will not mean it will generate the same structure and navigation when viewed via mobile. Web based engagement can impact a customer decision making process and shopping journey (Faulds et al. 2018), particularly in the form of mobile. For example, Amazon's mobile app harnesses the power of the website, and delivers a more convenient, and personalized experience. In the early days of mobile applications, apps were designed to simply mimic a website, and developers released deficient apps that did not incorporate essential navigation and engagement strategies. Today, we see far more powerful apps that are designed to better meet user's needs and contribute to a brands narrative in a consumer centric approach. More on Mobile in Chapter 4.

A website is built with hypertext markup language (HTML), and within this HTML are special tags, metatags. The metatags hold a lot of important information about the page content for search engines to index. A title tag is the tag that will display the first portion of your search engine results' listing. Title tags help to ensure listing on SERPS say the right things, contribute to click through rates, and also help search engines determine what the page is about. Be sure every page has a unique title and has no duplicates.

Off-page SEO strives to improve page ranking based on the quality of links coming to the site (Dodson 2016). When crafting content on a site, you will have the text that is within the page but also the hyperlinks embedded within the text. While internal links connect or link to other pages or other content within the same site, inbound links come from other websites to your website. The more links to you, the more "value" you are perceived to have, thus the higher your rankings will be.

Keywords are a significant word or phrase that relates to the content on your site (Dodson 2016). Keywords are directly related to SERP and should be strategic in their use on a webite by wat of content and meta-data. If a new mom was looking for a night nanny, relevant keywords for your site could be *new mom, nighttime nanny, reliable newborn nanny,* or the like. Search terms are commonly used phrases a user would enter in a search engine to find your site or business. In the past, these terms would have been two to four words, but with digital literacy rates much higher, longer terms are being used. Users know now the more specific the search, the more relevant the results. Optimizing content for keywords may also support building a positive brand image if you ensure the inclusion of keywords you want your brand to be associated with. To be successful, you must know what terms your customers use when searching for information related to your product or service. This again, necessitates a consumer centric marketing effort.

The content you house on your website is vital. This applies to blogs as well, we will explore blogs more fully in the next chapter. When people share your content across social networks, this is referred to as social sharing. This is facilitated by including social sharing buttons on your site. While a visitor may take the time to create a social media post and add your link to their social media, it is far more effective when the site has a simple "share" button that will populate all this information for the viewer, who then shares it on their social profile. This type of sharing is essentially free advertising for your organization, and this traffic is seen as quality content. Your branded and optimized content will help spread the word about your company or your brand and contribute to brand awareness. As you take the time to create content and ensure the user experience on your website is top notch, you must also drive consumers to it, and make it very easy for them to share it for you. The basic fundamentals surrounding on-page and off-page SEO must be part of any digital strategy to fully leverage the power behind Internet technologies.

While providing quality content is vital, it is still important to consider a solid link building strategy. Strategic link building contributes to brand awareness helping you gain a larger audience and build your brand. Effective traffic building has three aspects: targets, techniques, and timing (Chaffey and Smith 2017). Common traffic targets include quantity, quality, and cost of traffic. Generating traffic is not limited to driving visitor to your website, it may also include other third-party sites your target audience uses such as social networks or review pages. The techniques used include much of the content of this book such as e-mail, social media, search, online ads, and offline techniques such as direct mail, word of mouth, advertising, PR, and personal selling to name a few. And finally, timing. Traffic building campaigns can be tied to specific fixed durations.

The User Experience (UX) and Integrated Design

Once built, a website does not sit stagnant. Websites should always be kept up to date and used with strategic intent. Not only will you want to be updating the content, but also ensuring optimal functionality and an excellent customer experience. Consider the visitor who lands at your website, then leaves. Why did they not continue to click and look around? Was the navigation too difficult, was content they encountered not relevant? Did the image your brand portrays on the site not align with the visitor? There are several tools you might consider helping with the creation and maintenance of landing pages. A landing page simply refer to where the visitor lands after clicking a link from elsewhere (such as an e-mail, social post, or digital ad). This could be a dedicated landing page that is designed specifically around a particular campaign. Ideally, the visitor would find themselves on the landing page and perform some desired action such as subscribe if the landing page was set for subscribing. A home page can be a landing page, but it is not the best design. A landing page would be more specific, with a particular call to action for the visitor such as "subscribe" to the site, "download" a white paper, "learn more", or try for "free". If you need help tweaking your landing pages, there are several tools you could consider such as Hubspot Marketing Hub and Unbounce.

Consider the content you put on a website to also not be forever static, but instead always be evolving to ensure relevancy and easy sharing to other platforms such as social media and e-mail. The key is the inclusion of a call to action, and an embedded share button to go directly to the users' chosen platform. Infographics are a popular and effective use of owned media. These visual assets make it easy to share large amounts of data in an easy to consume form. Often, they are embedded in websites, blogs, or social media, and are easily shared by the user via social media such as LinkedIn, Twitter, Facebook, and Pinterest for example. Video is another owned media that is shared often and can garner great results, especially real-time video segments. Content you include on websites and blogs should always be considered for repurposing for other channels such as e-mail and social platforms.

We briefly touched on the idea of the customer journey earlier in our reading. Customer journey mapping is essential to the customer experience as it is central to data driven marketing (Lemon and Verhoef 2016). We explored this a bit within Chapter 1. Remember, during every stage of the process, a customer is comparing the experience you provide with those they have had in the past with your competitors. This is no different online, or off. In the context of this book, we will be exploring the journey and its connection to websites and peripheral digital channels. As part of this journey, we must understand expectations of service delivery, deliver on those expectations, while also accounting for customers engaging on multiple platforms offline and online. Organizations also need to ensure that security and privacy risks are minimized in order to fully participate in this relationship. When an organization is able to establish a safe and consistent presence over multiple platforms, it is in an essence meeting consumer where they are much like establishing presence in a physical space. The connections made across platforms, translates into the ability to guide and nurture your customers.

The various touchpoints within the customer journey map are sequential and they provide information on what is happening at each phase of this journey. At each point, there is data to be harnessed for more accurate data driven marketing decisions. Adding context to the data ensures you are adding relevance and value at each stage of the journey, while also ensuring you are taking a customer centric approach. By taking a customer centric marketing approach, marketers are better able to deliver optimal consumer experiences (Micheaux and Bosio 2019).

Listening to your audience online, is a simple, yet extremely effective way to ensure you keep the consumer front and center in all initiatives. When we think of the audience in this context, let us consider everyone, not just your existing customers, consider potential consumers, or even those who may influence other decision making. By listening, you will better understand them and really be able to initiate better conversations via digital platforms as well as ensure you understand what they care about and what is most important to them (as opposed to what *you* think is most important to them). Empower your customers, they will be more receptive if you approach all interactions with a choice on how they want to engage or communicate with you.

Excellent customer service via all digital channels should be a strategic objective for your organization. Customer satisfaction is known to be a recurrent relationship component (Blackston 2000), and detrimental to the idea of brand relationship. These interactions with the end consumer allow for tremendous opportunities to reinforce your brand, to build upon new and existing relationships, while also providing unique experiences for your customer. Long gone are the days where a customer would only reach out by phone or mailed letter. It is common for customers to now mention an organization by name online through social media, online reviews, or mobile application to share both joys and frustrations with a product or service. The degree of brand relationship becomes dependent on trust in the brand and customer satisfaction with the brand. It should be part of every brand's digital strategy to leverage mediums in a way that both contribute to trust and satisfaction in a proactive way.

A branded website should be where you are driving traffic with your digital marketing campaign. Often, brands will have a website that also includes a blog. Some smaller businesses may elect to simply have a blog as their main website. Over the last decade, it has become very common place to see a mixture of e-commerce and blogging on a branded website. As we have discussed, your digital marketing tools are used to engage with consumers, guide them through the customer journey, drive traffic to your website, and generate revenue. When a visitor enters your website, they arrive at a landing page. Landing page performance is detrimental to a digital marketing campaign. Once you have successfully driven web traffic to your website, it is the landing page's responsibility to persuade visitors to take a specific action. For example, you could have a page with a goal to have the visitor enter contact information, so they become leads, or you have a landing page design to persuade a visitor to make a purchase. There are many ways to design an effective landing page, and they may vary by brand. However, a rock-solid landing page only has one goal and has very little peripheral information or distractions. The focus of the page is solely on the action that you want the visitor to take. It is very straightforward, has clear focus, with the very few links in order to convert visitors into leads and sales.

Regardless of what type of landing page you have, they all must have a very clear call to action. For example, when it comes to a landing page design that can persuade a visitor to make a purchase, a clear call to action could be the button to click to add to cart. Conversely, if you have a landing page with the goal to have a visitor in your contact information to become a lead, you may have a call to action for the visitor to complete a lead form with contact information in exchange for white papers or a report. Worth noting, the more information you ask for in your form, the lower your conversion rate maybe.

Key Takeaways

The realm of search is not without its risks. There is somewhat of a lack of adequate technical skills surrounding search; there appears to be a wide digital skills gap in digital marketing (Aswani et al. 2018). There are also organizations that will be confronted with the decision of tackling search engine strategies in-house, or outsourcing. Should an organization decide to outsource this work, there needs to be consistency between the needs of the organization and the provider's competences.

To ensure a successful search engine strategy, significant investment is needed for the long run. SEO takes practice and a little experimentation and is an ongoing process. There is a lot of research to be done to really understand customer behavior and how to best ensure web content is relevant and valuable. This research will inform keywords and how you will drive traffic to your website through on-page and off-page SEO. Search engines such as Google, are important as they are typically the starting point for any consumer search. Whether a customer is searching for new shoes, a recipe, or service provider, they will typically begin with a Google search. It is important to note though, search marketing is not just about gaining traffic, the goal is still to move your customer from one stage of the customer journey to the next.

As we cover material in this book, you will see how each area of the umbrella of digital is needed to understand consumers, to reach them where they are in a meaningful way, and to do so at the right time with the right content. A digital strategy can be complex, with multiple tools being utilized. It is not uncommon for some professionals in digital to be an expert in one area but not another. We find many folks that work in SEO and SEM, who may not be as competent at writing copy for social. Just as we see some who may be a whiz at e-mail campaigns, but are not able to create a mobile app. All of the various areas of digital work together and should be part of one cohesive digital strategy that contributes to the brand and customer experience. In the following pages, we will dig a little deeper into how various digital assets can drive customers to your website and can help build your brand as a part of an integrated digital strategy.

CHAPTER 3

Social Media to Create and Nurture Relationships

Learning Objectives

- Analyze strategic use of social media for alignment with business objectives as part of an integrated digital strategy.
- Understand the connection between blogging, storytelling, and branding.
- Identify strengths and weaknesses of social media and associated tools for reaching and engaging target audiences.

In today's competitive and global market, social media is an instrumental tool for organizations to engage in two-way conversations with consumers. Social media refers to platforms such as Facebook and Twitter, video sharing sites such as YouTube and Vimeo, weblogs (also known as blogs), photo sharing sites like Instagram, and brand-hosted forums similar to the Dell Community or Amazon's product review pages (Rogers 2017). Utilizing these platforms (among many others) to communicate a brand message (brand-generated content) to the consumer is only one facet of social media marketing. Social media includes virtual platforms that allow users to not only create and share information, but to also exchange information in a multitude of formats. Social media adds benefits to organizations by generating value in relationships and networks (Drummond et al. 2020). Brands now include the generation of timely and relevant content via social media platforms as part of strategic marketing initiatives. Consumers are also creating and sharing content (user-generated content) on these platforms, effectively contributing to the branding of products and services, while also contributing to virtual communities surrounding brands (Rogers 2017). Social media, and their respective networks, have developed into a tool to influence consumers and have become ingrained in daily life for most consumers. Social media marketing activities are playing a vital role in building brand loyalty and are a key antecedent of brand loyalty (Ahmed et al. 2019).

The objectives for a social media campaign should be decided upon prior to delving into the social media groundswell. For example, consider key objectives such as to increase sales, brand awareness, customer acquisition, or customer retention. Along with objectives, considerations on how to measure the success of the campaign should be outlined. Goals should be matched with associated key performance indicators (KPIs), and metrics should be identified to properly evaluate social media initiatives. Social media as we know it now is far different than it was several years ago, and it will very likely be quite different in the coming years. It will evolve due to the constant innovation in technology and the evolution of how consumers of social media use social platforms (Pandley et al. 2020).

Social media has changed the ways in which brands reach and communicate with consumers. Additionally, social media has forever changed the way consumers communicate with one another and communicate with brands. Social media is becoming less about the technologies or the platforms (Appel et al. 2020), and more about the relationships created and nurtured within them. Consumers are on the platforms adding to the narratives every day. User-generated content is just one of the facets of social media. Consider that every day, people from all over the globe create this content by way of updating their Facebook status, tweeting about a product or service, sharing and commenting on YouTube videos, posting online reviews, publishing blog posts, and more. All of this content is consumed and shared through online social networks, which creates virtual communities of consumers and brands (Rogers 2017). Such user-generated content related to brands, helps shape what consumers think about a particular brand and can even impact brand awareness. All of this is multiplied exponentially when harnessed with brand-generated content into one integrated approach, directly impacting the consumer experience.

Engagement on social media platforms influences brand loyalty in a variety of contexts. Brand generated content helps a brand tell a narrative, or story, to not only help engage with consumers, but to also mold the perceptions of the brand. As part of this narrative, we see user-generated content also contributing to this brand story. Strategic and intentional use of the right social media strategies can help brands meet customers where they are online, create quality relationships, and increase brand loyalty. In fact, user-generated content is perceived as more trustworthy by consumers than any other marketing communication. Thus, if brands can effectively utilize user-generated content, they will be able to build brand trust and loyalty. The notion of creating and maintaining relationships with consumers is a proven relationship marketing business strategy. It is also one that can be improved upon with including the right mix of social platforms, for the right circumstances, at the right times. Lest we not forget, creating and nurturing brand relationships in a transparent and authentic way is absolutely vital. Kotler et al. (2017) suggest authenticity to be one of the most valuable assets for a brand.

Many brands already utilize social media platforms as a place to provide care for customers and connect with customers in both synchronous and asynchronous environments. Customers are able to engage with organizations anywhere and anytime, and brands are able to more fully engage with problems and offer solutions. The average consumer has quickly embraced social media as a way to get a brand's attention with a public complaint. It has become much easier to create a tweet or comment via Facebook describing a service failure, rather than call via telephone and wait for the next customer service representative. However, it is not uncommon for a customer service issue projected via social media to not be addressed. Given this scenario, the consumer will likely have a more negative attitude toward the brand. It is also likely that this service failure will be shared multiple times via digital platforms mimicking negative word of mouth, but with a much larger audience. At times, brands may be tempted to delete extremely negative posts, however deleting such feedback can generate further negative actions and is typically not the best way to handle the comments. As we have seen throughout the text, engaging in online conversations with consumers lends itself to establishing authenticity. Keeping all the comments, both good and bad, is a solid strategy as long as the negative comments do not violate terms of service and other set guidelines. Deleting negative comments will also further anger a consumer, leading to likely more negative complements and a larger customer service issue.

Alternatively, there are many benefits to meeting consumer expectations when engaging via social media broadcast service failures. For example, if the issue is addressed in a timely manner. This communicates to the consumer that they are important, and their issue is important to you. This is one way to show that your brand cares and wants to help. This is your opportunity as a brand to show your value to a consumer. Instead of viewing negative feedback as 'negative', embrace it. The idea of service recovery should be top of mind. With this feedback, consumers have in effect given your brand a second chance. It may be possible to salvage the relationship, but those managing social media accounts must aim to exceed and not simply meet expectations. Addressing social media posts provides your brand the opportunity to exceed expectations in the handling of the customer service complaint. Oftentimes consumers will take this positive and swift interaction and in turn recommend the brand through social media. These consumers tend to have a high probabilty of becoming a more loyal consumer. In this scenario, you have shown you are responsive to the consumers needs, and the consumer can count on you to make it right.

In the past, service failures were handled discreetly by customer service departments, now we see these same customer service interactions broadcast on social media platforms. Given the public nature of social media, these service failures may result in the loss of loyal consumers and impact the relationships with others exposed to the interactions between a disgruntled consumer and the organization (Melancon and Dalakas 2018). Organizations can facilitate customer service-related issues by way of chat bots and virtual assistants. These methods provide a much quicker response by being economically scalable for many brands (Appel et al. 2020). However, automation can result in a loss of compassion and empathy that "real" persons can provide. Thus, social media dialogue needs to be extremely authentic and personalized to the issue. Fully leveraging social media and all of its assets in an authentic way, will help reduce the need for call centers and reduce pain points for consumers, while also increasing convenience for customers.

Social media, when used effectively, can help marketers build relationships with consumers. Additionally, social platforms can also help build relationships between consumers themselves, thus, leading to creating a sense of community overall. This is paramount for brands to understand as they work to create consistent brand messages, and continually contribute to the brand narrative in a systematic way via these platforms. Sharing information via social media can build relationships, as social media encourages engagement that is needed in order to cultivate strong relationships. Important to this process is the idea of social media listening tools to ensure you are actively listening and following up on the various social mentions of your organization and or brand on social platforms. These tools are effective for staying on top of what consumers are saying, what the competition is saying, and other related conversations that you may wish to follow.

There are approximately 2.4 billion conversations going on about a brand online everyday (Melancon and Dalakas 2018). It stands to reason that marketers must absolutely understand and have strategies for customer service issues in order to both maintain and nurture consumer relationships. With effective and timely monitoring of social media networks, brands are better able to solve service or product issues in a timely fashion. This also allows for the cultivation of customers who are advocates of the brand to provide testimonials (Achen 2017), or be involved in other areas of a brand's marketing such as consumer research. There are ways to take a pulse on your audience and utilize this information for strategic planning and decision making, as well as agile pivots. Multiple tools exist to do so, ranging from free to paid, and finding a solution is dependent on goals and budget. While social media listening has long been used to better understand what consumers are saying in the space, not all customers are comfortable with brands listening in. Those who are not receptive to being listened to via social media may develop a negative attitude and loss of trust, further complicating the landscape for marketers. The brands that can overcome these hurdles are able to do so by proactively having plans in place for those scenarios, as well as looking at negative situations as opportunities to convert the negative into a positive.

There is an enormous amount of data available to marketers due to the prolific use of social media. Marketers are leveraging this data for strategic insights and digital marketing (Jacobson et al. 2020). Brands can use this information to inform a variety of initiatives with optics into consumers provided by analytics, and also through focus groups or interviews within social media communities. For example, social listening tools help uncover what consumers are "talking" about in the space, tools exist to search keywords in the social spaces, and sentiment analysis can be done as well. All of these tools are adding depth to our decision making as marketers and they offer qualitative and quantitative means to collect the data needed to make better business decisions. However, much like any other formal or informal marketing research, there are plenty of opportunities for error (Tuten and Soloman 2018). Not to mention lurking privacy issues, and the importance of considering consumers' concerns and integrating them into a marketer's practices moving forward (Jacobson et al. 2020).

Blogging as Part of the Social Media Mix

Blogging is one of the most powerful tools in your digital marketing toolbelt, thus an entire section devoted to devoted to blogging is included as opposed to outlining opposed to outlining all the popular social platforms of the day. Each brand and business will find value in various platforms depending on the target audience, that will be for each to determine. However, platforms should integrate with a website and/or blog regardless of the platforms chosen. Much like websites in the prior chapter, blogs can tie together the various branded elements of the digital landscape. A blog is another umbrella term to describe an online space where one posts new content on a regular basis, it is a shortened form of web log, whereas business blogging is a marketing tactic that utilizes a blog to increase visibility online and is considered to be an additional marketing channel to support business growth and add value for the consumer.

A blog site will house such content as articles, images, audio, and video, and in today's digital landscape, many business websites will include a blogging section. Consider the idea of inbound marketing and how important a repository of content is to a brand. Also consider the importance of a central location that ties all social and digital channels together. A blog can not only generate awareness but can also become a critical and central part of your digital marketing mix. However, if done without a strategic approach and without a "big picture" view, a blog can become a very time-consuming task that creates little if any return on investment.

Blogs can stand alone, but they are traditionally a section of the business website. While many brands tie a blog to their overall marketing editorial calendar, it also offers the freedom to publish content on the fly. The idea is to create original content that will allow the brand to rank on search engines for a variety of keywords and to support the customer decision-making process by offering content that answers questions that consumers often have about a product or service.

Blog posts should answer a consumer's questions or solve a particular problem for the reader, and also strive to engage the target audience in a solution. Using keywords within your blogging strategy enables you to drive a fair amount of organic search toward your main website if content and keywords align with what consumers are searching for on search engines. You can use the same SEO (search engine optimization) tactics or paid advertising that you do on websites on a blog. Providing this valuable information that consumers seek, not only creates brand awareness but can also create the idea of community and build relationships.

When crafting the blog post, your title, body text, image text and meta-description all contribute to your SEO. Another excellent way to optimize your blog is to include hyperlinks to other articles associated with the content at hand. You can link to articles within the same blog site, or external resources. These hyperlinks not only add to your SEO, but also offer the reader the opportunity to click on links to further explore the ideas in your blog post. Always keep your reader in mind. If you address a topic within your blog post that the average reader may not understand, link to a resource that explains it. Again, this link could be to your own content or another site you were not associated with but offers relevant information on the topic. Also often overlooked is categorization of blog posts. Including categories on your blog site helps to improve the user experience and add value for the reader. Ideally, you want your Blog site to be easily navigated, as well as the individual blog posts.

If SEO is done properly within your social media blog post, your post will rank higher in search engines (such as Google) than other content. If content from your blog is shared on your other social platforms in meaningful and valuable ways, this will drastically improve your chances of having content discovered by your specified target audience. A blog post should be optimized via the utilization of relevant keywords or keyword phrases. Blogging platforms such as WordPress offer the ability to easily address SEO, as long as it's not overlooked. WordPress offers both free and paid sites, the paid site offering significantly more options for optimization. WordPress is extremely user-friendly and search engine friendly, allowing for multiple users with various levels of permission, and integration with other social platforms.

A blog needs to be updated frequently, creating new content in the form of posts that engage the audience. This engagement can come in many forms, such as sharing on social media or commenting. And, much like a website, a blog should offer clear and simple navigation for users, and also digitally connected to other social networks like Facebook, Twitter, Instagram, and the like where links can be easily shared, and hashtags formulated to contribute to online conversations. A blog can truly leverage the power of social sharing, therefore social media sharing buttons and widgets should always be front and center within communications regardless if on a website, blog, or e-mail. This encourages your audience to share via their social media platforms. A blog harnesses is the power of a website but offers the additional benefit of conversation. Marketing managers should plan to share interesting, informative, and media rich content to create a memorable experience for the consumer (Beig and Khan 2018). Content you include on websites and blogs should always be considered for repurposing for other channels such as e-mail and social platforms. With crafting several types of content that relate to specific topics, visitors can easily transition from one piece of content to the next, becoming more familiar with your brand and its offerings.

Posts should be easy to digest, purposeful, add value, and resonate with the reader. Successful blog posts typically will tell a story and will guide the reader through story telling. An effective writing strategy for blogs is to guide the reader through the content of your post through a story. While the main points of your blog post will have meaning, they will have more traction if delivered via storytelling. Blog readers seek out information and practical tips to help them solve a problem or to make their lives easier. With including a story woven throughout the blog post, you will be able to present that material in a format that is very easily digestible and remembered. Humans are hardwired to crave a good story, in fact history tells us our ancestors used this technique to pass down life lessons, educate young people and entertain one another. Don't we all remember Aesop's Fables? Storytelling via digital offers unique opportunities to connect in meaningful ways with consumers. Good storytelling grabs our attention and leaves us wanting to know what happens next.

Do not underestimate the value of formatting within a blog post as well. Readers tend to skim; therefore, it is necessary to include visual elements such as white space, headings, font changes, images, bullets, and lists. An affective blog post also includes some form of a call to action. What more do you want the reader to do upon reading? Do you want them to click to comment, click to share, or subscribe via e-mail? Keep the conversation going. A blog post has many goals, such as branding and providing valuable information to your audience. However, do not lose sight that a blog should also generate quality leads that ultimately lead to a sale.

Blogposts should capture your brand personality. Just as your social media posts on Twitter should capture your unique perspective, articles should do the same. Consistency is key in digital marketing— Consistency in marketing message, consistency in personality, consistency in images, consistency in all areas of your approach on all platforms. According to Aaker (1996), the idea of brand personality in quantitative and qualitative studies is not uncommon and is in fact interpretable and consistent across populations. When you think of the brands you buy, can you categorize them by strong personality or lack thereof based on the messaging you receive? Do you perceive some brands as more youthful and fun, while others may be more dependable and rugged? As you craft your content (regardless of platform), it is imperative to capture this personality in a consistent, and authentic way.

After your blog posts are live and have been promoted via social platforms, it does not end there. We will delve more into measuring success at the end of this book, but keep in mind, looking at which blog posts have the most comments or have been shared the most may indicate potential opportunities. There may be an opportunity to create a multipart series to more deeply address a specific topic that is popular with readers. There may also be the opportunity to repurpose content published previously. Perhaps you had a popular blog post that could inform a YouTube video or podcast episode.

Bloggers can be identified as influencers as well, given those with large followings do have the capability to shape consumer opinion as well as drive traffic to brands. It is not uncommon for an Instagram influencer to have an associated blog, or vice versa. Influencers interact, communicate, and engage on many digital platforms, most commonly on Instagram and YouTube, but influencers are also found within Twitter, Facebook, LinkedIn, Snapchat, and TikTok (Slijepčević et al. 2020). The strategic approach with presence on multiple social platforms ensures their visibility and often attracts brands to them specifically for that reach. Bloggers and influencers are major players for promoting a brand and associated promotion of products and services. The idea of an influencer is not a new one, word of mouth (WOM) marketing has always had significant influence on opinion and consumers, and has consistently played a role in communications due to the credibility that it provides (Coll and Micó 2019). Word of mouth is just one of the important characteristics that sets the digital landscape apart from the traditional marketing landscape. Consumers are able to share information not only with close friends, but with complete strangers on a variety of social networks (Kannan and Li 2017), both positive and negative. Exchanges are made via online forums, review sites, websites, and social media providing a rapid and largescale sharing of (potentially negative) word of mouth that has the ability to reach substantially large networks of consumers. The Word of Mouth Marketing Association (WOMMA) defines an influencer as one who has a greater than average scope or impact in relevant markets, and influencer marketing as the process of identifying and communicating with influencers in support of a business objective (Word of Mouth Marketing Association [WOMMA] 2010). Online word of mouth is seen to have a larger volume then offline word of mouth given it is much more accessible and can be shared more widely within the digital landscape (Kannan and Li 2017). According to the Association of National Advertisers (ANA), influencer marketing leverages "individuals who have influence over potential buyers and orienting marketing activities around these individuals to drive a brand message to the larger market" (American Marketing Association 2020).

An influencer is often compensated to promote associated brands. Influencers are becoming, in some instances, the face of brands (Slijepčević et al. 2020). The last several years have seen a rise in influencer marketing and associated policy as well. Brands are utilizing influencers to promote different products or services while interacting, communicating, and engaging with target audiences on behalf of the brand. Ideally, influencer marketing would be combined with other marketing communications where content is strategically leveraged. It is worth noting that coordination between marketing teams is important should collaboration be part of a strategic approach. It is possible that influencers for major brands will continue to be prolific, however, these traditional celebrities are relatively expensive for smaller brands. Therefore, we have seen the emergence of the micro-influencer. While they may not be as well-known as A-list celebrities, they typically have an enthusiastic following and are generally considered to be more trustworthy and authentic than traditional celebrities.

Strategic Use of Social Media as Part of an Integrated Digital Strategy

Virtually every part of a consumer's decision-making process is somehow intersecting with social media influence (Appel et al. 2020). We explored this within Chapter 1 as we reflected on a simple Google search, we know social media posts are listed within the search engine results and we also know that consumers value the input of friends, family, peers, and other consumers when making such decisions. Consider how often Yelp may be consulted when making a purchase decision, or even the idea of watching reviews and unboxing videos for particular products on YouTube by influencers and micro-influencers. The idea of consumers watching live experiences has become quite common, and popular. For example, live streaming of video games on Twitch, and even livestreaming on Facebook to include question and answer sessions, special product launches or announcements, or even behind-the-scenes video for loyal fans and audiences. The idea of virtual influencers that look much like a human, will become more prominent in social media in the coming years. Some brands have already been experimenting with the use of virtual influencers, blending influencer marketing with artificial intelligence. Virtual influencers are engaging as they can combine on point messaging, lower risk, and embrace personalities that are crafted to mirror the brand's values. Such scenarios illustrate the importance of social media and how influential they can be within the consumer decision-making process. Social media influences e-commerce in all five of the customer decision-making stages (Tuten and Soloman 2018).

Social media content can be a powerful driver traffic to your organization's website. Social media updates typically will include a blurb of content and hyperlink back to your website. As the social media post is crafted, it is paramount for the brand personality to shine through. Think of the stark differences between a brand tied to law-enforcement or government versus one focused on children's recreation. One is drastically more formal than the other. If you were to craft social media posts for one and share on the other, there would be a complete misalignment. A brand tied to law-enforcement or government should have a more formal tone than one related to children's recreation. Social media updates or posts have significant value in providing information to current and prospective customers.

Social media has become one of the most important strategic tools for digital marketers, not only to share brand messages, but also to help create and maintain long-term brand loyalty (Rogers 2017). Social media platforms are now a necessary marketing tool for brands to reach specific target audiences and marketing managers are increasingly recognizing the immense value and importance of social media marketing to establish relationships with consumers. On these same platforms, consumers are creating and sharing their own content (user-generated content), thus contributing to the branding of consumer products and services, while also contributing to virtual communities surrounding brands (Rogers 2017). Customers who join online brand communities via social media can support a brand in product development while also becoming key in providing valuable feedback. This also nourishes the idea of brand loyalty and allows the customer to become a co-creator along with the brand. If marketers broaden our view of loyalty to include relative attitude and peripheral contingencies, there can be a much stronger direction that highlights appropriate strategic alternatives (Dick and Basu 1994). This in turn does help inform strategic direction for a host of initiatives in the digital landscape.

Social media has changed integrated marketing communication strategy (IMC), and as such marketers must account for the differences between social media and traditional media channels. Because of the uniqueness of social media, this particular platform can be used within an integrated campaign to engage and interact with customers instead of just a tool to share information (Achen 2017). Social media marketing can help brands create, nurture, and build relationships with consumers, as well as help build relationships and opportunities for engagement between consumers themselves, leading to creating a sense of community. Consider the consumer who reaches out to a brand via social media concerning a customer service issue. This allows for somewhat direct discussions on what the problem is and how one might fix it. It is not uncommon for these inquires, when solved, result in a significantly stronger relationship between brand and consumer (and increase in purchases) because of this interaction. This interaction might also even uncover an anticipated need of your consumers, giving direction for future initiatives for your organization. It is worth noting that with all of the possibilities with social media in regards to marketing, there's still a gap in the understanding customers comfort with marketing's use of the data produced by social media (Jacobson et al. 2020).

It is obvious social media is an important part of the marketing process. However, social media are different than our traditional media and thus require new metrics for measurement. While the number of likes and followers are popular measures of the reach of a brand, standing alone they are not an adequate measure of consumer engagement or relationship strength, they are purely vanity metrics. Not to mention, the implementation of social and digital strategies can bring additional complexities that require a new way of thinking in many areas (Drummond, O'Toole and McGrath 2020). A central issue with social media is the lack of a definitive and widely accepted definition of what customer engagement really is, there are several definitions floating around. What does engagement with your brand mean to you? Is it simply a comment, a "like" ? Measuring the impact of engagement means you must have clearly defined what engagement means to you. There are cognitive, emotional, and behavioral aspects to engagement, it will be paramount to clearly define what engagement is for the purposes of your strategic digital approach.

While your organization's budget may not match those of leading brands on social media such as Starbucks or Spotify, you may be able to learn from their campaigns. Paying special attention to the content that is shared, the tactics they use, and their unique approaches, you may be able to implement some of the same tactics on a smaller scale depending on your objectives.

Key Takeaways

Social media provides a structure for social interactions between brands and consumers and between consumers themselves (Tuten and Soloman 2018). Users communicate around content provided by brands and users alike, to create and contribute to a narrative. As we look to the future of social media, it's imperative to expand the perspectives beyond of social media and consider how consumers of social media platforms might use these mediums (Appel et al. 2020).

Social is a key component of an effective Marketing strategy on a multitude of fronts, however, the ability to harness the power of social media does not come without risks. While allowing consumers and brands alike to contribute to this narrative, it opens the doors for negative comments, negative perceptions, and sticky situations as well. As we have learned, service failures are on full display via social media. Negative consumer comments and interactions have led many organizations to fear social media and not understand how to address such issues. It is no wonder many brands avoid interacting with negative comments on social media given the backlash from consumers and associated bad press, and often falling stock prices.

As new social platforms emerge, marketer must strive to understand the types of interactions that exist within them, and how those may be leveraged and integrated with the organization's overarching goals and vision. Given how quickly the social media environment changes and evolves, it becomes quite challenging for marketers to accurately measure the value of investments in these particular channels. However, from an extremely broad perspective, social media can help organizations meet relationship marketing goals when they are strategically used to uncover customer needs, increase satisfaction, and enhance relationship value (Achen 2017). Marketers crafting social media strategies around building relationships is just one way to ensure you are adding value for your customers. The notion of engagement on social media should include not only measures for interacting, but for offline integration of content as well. Social is an integral part of an integrated marketing communication strategy.

CHAPTER 4

Mobile and E-Mail as Part of the Customer Experience

Learning Objectives

- Analyze strategic use of mobile technology as part of an integrated digital strategy.
- Determine appropriate mobile marketing tactics that align with an organization's larger marketing strategy.
- Understand how mobile and e-mail contribute to the customer experience.
- Analyze strategic use of e-mail as part of an integrated digital strategy.

Consider both your professional and personal lives, and how a smart phone has embedded itself into your daily life. Smartphones are used for informational, entertainment, purchasing, banking, and communication purposes (Keller 2013), allowing the access of information just about anything, at any time. We share much more about ourselves than we have done before, we take photos and then share on social media, posting video content to video sharing sites, utilizing apps for entertainment or specific tasks while providing a plethora of data to the provider. The mobile phone, or smart phone as we know it today, has changed human behavior and thus how we market.

Mobile marketing is considered a multichannel online marketing technique that focuses on reaching targeted audiences via smartphone, tablet, or related devices by e-mail, website, SMS and MMS, social media or mobile application (Kolekar et al. 2018). The prevalence of mobile device use by consumers has made shopping a continuous rather than a discrete activity. This ultimately requires businesses to engage with consumers at critical touchpoints of the decision process, providing a more customer centric experience (Faulds et al. 2018). Mobile devices, excluding tablets, generate about half of all website traffic globally (Hubspot 2020b).

While this presents many opportunities, it presents a host of challenges as well. Given the variety of devices that allow consumers to access online offerings, such as computers smartphones, tablets, and connected TV's, the decision-making process and purchase process becomes not only more versatile but also extremely complex (Wagner et al. 2020). The customer experience both online and offline are creating many touchpoints with consumers, thus an omnichannel approach is imperative to embrace to ensure customer interactions are consistent across all channels, on and offline.

Just as we have changed as consumers, marketers have adapted as well. Marketing has moved beyond the traditional 4P's and AIDA (awareness, interest, desire, action) to include fundamental shifts in how we define our target audiences, how we produce meaningful encounters with consumers, and how we approach the consumer decision making process (understanding they now control the dialogue more than brands). Mobile gives consumers a sense that they are in control of the decision-making process, resulting in a more informed yet demanding consumer. This new connected customer does not move through the traditional AIDA model in a straight path. They are online searching reviews, listening to peers, reaching out to brands at every stage of the purchasing process, thus making the decision-making process significantly more complex than it was in the past. Mobile technologies empower the consumer in the decision-making process; this process is now an integrative process that results in more personalized interactions (Faulds et al. 2018).

Mobile has given businesses the opportunity to more actively influence the consumer decision-making process as a whole, rather than focused primarily on the idea of purchase versus non purchase (Faulds et al. 2018). Mobile has become a significant focus of marketers in order to understand the benefits that consumers gain from each of the channels. This helps to determine effective and efficient strategies that ensure a consumer-centric strategy. Mobile shopping has been revolutionized with the ability for brands to identify the geographical location of consumers, then target them with customized communications. Geotargeting allows marketers to take advantage of the digital landscape to send messaging to consumers based on location and what they may be engaging in (Keller 2013). Geographical location combined with other data can influence a consumer's decision-making process. Through strategically crafted messages and marketing tactics, marketers are able to deliver an extremely personalized experience.

A mobile strategy takes form only after you have established objectives and goals are identified for your mobile channel. Just as any other strategy, goals and objectives for mobile should be related to the overall business objectives for your organization. Consider how mobile will help you achieve these objectives; consider how you are able to impact the consumer experience with mobile technology. Just as any marketing strategy, you need to understand your existing customers, new customers, and your target. Determining the right approach for meeting these objectives is important before you take any technical steps toward your mobile strategy.

In order to implement a successful mobile strategy, it is paramount to ensure your website is set up for mobile. There are many automated systems that can offer this service for you, they will take your existing website content and format it to fit mobile screens. WordPress offers plugins that do this, however, there are other companies that are able to create a separate mobile website completely independent from your main website. Refer back to Chapter 2 for additional content on an optimized site and ensuring the user experience within that site is enhanced. Having your website optimized for mobile simply means consumers will be able to interact with your mobile application much like they would on your website. Navigation should be easy to follow, transactions should be streamlined, and all elements of design should be consumer centric.

You will also want to ensure you have claimed your business on location-based apps and platforms, like Facebook Places and the once hugely popular Foursquare. Facebook Places is a geolocation feature on Facebook that allows users to check into certain locations with their mobile phones. This becomes extremely important if you have brick and mortar locations. Claiming your business on these platforms is the equivalent of making sure you are listed in a phone directory. These platforms will allow you to run mobile promotions. For example, you may be able to utilize Facebook to offer discounts or perks to visitors who quote "check in" to your location. Uber and Pokémon Go are also considered location-based applications. These location-based applications are essentially facilitating two-way communication between the user, and the service provider. The user is transmitting data related to their location and preferences to the provider. With emerging technologies such as AR and VR, we will see these apps further leveraged for consumer behavior and research surrounding trend. As we see advances in analytics and big data, we will likely see a significant boost in their functionality.

QR (quick response) codes have been around for some time, but we started seeing more of them during the Pandemic in 2020. Restaurants offered bare bones setups at tables, no salt and pepper shakers or menus to be used multiple times between cleanings. Instead, restaurants placed only signage with their QR code for patrons to scan. Upon scanning the QR barcode, information including the menu populates. Not only was this easy for restaurant goers, it eliminated the need to reuse menus between customers. QR codes drive consumers to mobile webpages with specific content such as coupons, special offers, or a menu in the case of my example earlier. QR codes are very simple to use, you as a customer would simply open your camera and your smart phone will read the QR code. There are also several apps that serve as QR code readers. The creation of a QR code is quite simple as well, there are several services online that will do this for you. Uses for QR codes are endless, but you will typically see QR codes on printed material and on websites. QR codes are even being used by street artists to earn tips via crypto currencies.

As part of a mobile strategy, you will want to run a mobile advertising campaign. There are several popular mobile advertising platforms such as AdMob from Google or iAd from Apple. With these tools you can create a mobile advertisement based on cost per click, cost per thousand, or cost per acquisition. Imagine a pop-up ad on mobile when a user enters in a search that aligns with your business offerings. These mobile advertising platforms offer actionable insights and are quite easy to use to help you grow your business.

Mobile accounts for approximately 46 percent of all e-mail openings (Hubspot 2020a). Mobile is quickly becoming a preferred method for opening e-mail, depending on the age group. Mobile plays a huge role in e-mail marketing with mobile users able to access e-mail from anywhere at any time through e-mail apps and phone set up features. E-mail is not just sent via desktop, it finds its way to laptops, tablets, smartphone and even through an Alexa in your kitchen. With this, marketers must be sure to keep subject lines short and to the point in order for this to display on a mobile device. Developing content with mobile in mind ensures your e-mail strategy performs as expected. The e-mail experience has changed the user experience, and it continues to evolve due to mobile technology.

In order to fully understand what mobile marketing is and what you are able to do, you need to be sure that you immerse yourself in the mobile landscape as a consumer. For example, consider your favorite apps on your smartphone. How familiar are you with their design and navigation? Utilize some of these apps to inform purchasing decisions, facilitate communication, or pay for your next Starbucks with their mobile payment app and earn rewards through their loyalty program. The more you use mobile, the more you will see that it is pretty straightforward and simply another marketing channel for consumers. The key is to enhance the customer experience in a meaningful way, and in a way that adds value for your end user.

Using E-Mail to Drive Sales and Keep Customers Interested

E-mail remains one of the most effective ways to reach and communicate your brand's message to a specific individual or group of individuals. It is consistently ranked among the most effective marketing channels, outperforming social media, affiliate marketing, and SEO. E-mail may be so effective given the average consumer uses e-mail more than any of the other digital platforms. E-mail marketing facilitates conversion of browsers to buyers and can support the decision-making process along the way. There is a significant ROI (return in investment) with e-mail marketing. In fact, e-mail generates approximately $38 for every $1 dollar spent, translating into about a 3,800 percent ROI (HubSpot 2020). Additionally, 87 percent of business to business (B2B) marketers say e-mail is one of their top free organic distribution channels (Content Marketing Institute 2020). In addition, e-mail also reaches the mobile user as we saw earlier in this chapter, in effect giving your brand more bang for your buck. E-mail is one of the most commonly used mobile applications, accounting for 46 percent of all e-mail opens (Litmus 2018). And finally, e-mail marketing campaigns are quite easy to measure. There are established metrics such as opens, clicks, and click through rates (CTR).

E-mail allows you to engage in one to one communication much like we do with direct mail advertisements to a consumer's home. However, with e-mail you can verify if the message was received, opened, and read. Whereas with direct mail, you would have no idea if the mailing was viewed. Including e-mail as part of your digital marketing strategy offers you the opportunity to leverage the power of relationship-based marketing. The key is to utilize the right type of e-mail at the right time. Traditionally, there are three types of e-mails: transactional, relational, and promotional e-mails. Transactional e-mails are sent to customer who have either made an order or have engaged with your brand in some capacity. Transactional e-mails typically re-engage consumers and offer you the opportunity to fully present your brand voice and personality. Relational e-mails offer customers information such as a newsletter blog article or the like (remember those visitors to your website who opted in due to your effective landing page!). These types of e-mails offer something of value for the consumer. And finally, promotional e-mails typically present both leads and customers with a specified offer. Promotional e-mails are the most common type of marketing e-mail sent by brands. These types of e-mails are particularly useful for lead generation, loyalty, nurturing relationship, sales, and retention.

Often, brands will rely heavily on one format of e-mails without consideration of the other styles. Consider how this looks to a consumer. Using a combination of the three e-mails can help build a relationship between the brand and consumer. These e-mail transactions speak to the primary goal of marketing, as well as contribute to the overall customer service experience. E-mail can also contribute to brand awareness, generating leads, engage or re-engage consumers, and aid retention and loyalty. However, not all e-mail types have the same open rates.

E-mail is typically used as part of a welcome program and is a necessary part of establishing and investing in the relationship with a consumer. Your first interaction should be well thought out, and targeted.

Ensure you have enough information about the consumer and you know and understand their needs and expectations. Do you know where is this e-mail lead is coming from? Is this in response to content related to a free offering, more information, or is this an existing customer support inquiry? Knowing these details will enable you to have a more meaningful interaction with the customer. An effective e-mail strategy can welcome, nurture, and encourage them to buy, as well as entice those who may have strayed to come back to you. Consider your own personal online shopping habits. How often have you abandoned your shopping cart and did not check out? What if the brand e-mailed you some time after with a nice message to remind you to check out, or remind you of stock levels, or even remind you along with a current discount code?

Just as the other digital marketing tools we've covered thus far, e-mail has its place in your overall strategy. As you craft blog posts and social media posts, you will also include an e-mail strategy that presents a cohesive experience for the customer. If your e-mail messages are crafted correctly and sent at the right time, they have the ability to engage customers and contribute to the customer journey. A promotional calendar offers the opportunity to plan ahead and offer the right message at the right time, often coordinated with a blog editorial calendar and other content distribution channels. It becomes tricky when trying to create an e-mail campaign that not only moves customers through their customer journey, but also creates long-term engagement and loyalty, and ensure you do so without becoming annoying and irritating to customers. Simply because a consumer opts into your e-mail list, that does not mean they are fully engaged with your brand. You need to build a relationship, one where a consumer understands the value you can provide and what to expect from you. Just like a blog post, the writing and designing of an effective e-mail can make or break your campaign. If you want a customer or lead to open and read your e-mail, the copy and the design are important, as well as the inclusion of a call to action. In order to craft an effective e-mail copy, ensure you understand why a customer would engage with a particular promotion. You need to address the target audience, address how your product or service will impact her life, show evidence of your claims, and include reference to why your particular e-mail is timely. Understanding why people buy allows you to harness consumer motivations and what drives your customers.

Never underestimate the power of a subject line! Consider most people only glanced at their e-mail and will delete it immediately if they do not see value or a subject line that grabs their attention. There is nothing more disheartening than crafting a wonderful e-mail and subject line to send to a specified target audience, and your open rate hovers around 10 percent. And even worse, you see many unsubscribe requests in response to your clever e-mail. Hudak et al. (2017) found that in most cases, recipients of e-mail viewed the first 3 words of the subject line, and the majority of respondents read four words at most, highlighting the need for affective subject lines. Understanding the nuances of consumer behavior within e-mail is important to ensure conversions.

It is not uncommon for e-mail marketing campaigns to have low clickthrough rates, however it is important to consider an e-mail marketing strategy that optimizes the location or placement of links in order to facilitate drawing the attention of the consumer and hopefully increasing the numbers of clicks. If the goal of your e-mail marketing strategy is to drive website traffic to specific page or influence a purchase decision, then link placement becomes critical. Interestingly, links located on the left side of an e-mail newsletter, are more likely to be clicked than those in other locations. Further, the sheer number of links and length of the e-mail can have positive effects on clickthrough rates, however, do you keep the content of the e-mail somewhat succinct, with very few redundancies (Kumar and Salo 2018).

Another consideration is that many consumers today have a main e-mail address they will share with their contacts, and another e-mail they provide to retailers and possibly "spammy" folks. It is paramount to show consumers and leads you are not a spammer, and you have something of value for them. Also consider many of the Internet and e-mail service providers can automatically move your e-mail into a spam folder. Your goal in an e-mail marketing campaign is to ensure your e-mail does not come off as spam so that e-mail deliverability is not impacted. The CAN-SPAM Act of 2003 (FTC 2020) outlines requirements for businesses utilizing e-mail marketing. Some of the noteworthy requirements include honoring opt-out (unsubscribing) requests in prompt manner, include such information on how to opt out clearly in the e-mail, include your location, identify the e-mail as an advertisement, and do not use false or misleading subject lines.

Effective use of e-mail marketing is largely dependent on relevancy. Ensuring your e-mail is relevant to the intended target is key as in irrelevant e-mail may be ignored, or worse, prompt the target to unsubscribe. Knowing you target audience (who may or may not be a current consumer depending on your goals and the campaign), ensures you are relevant, and your message is more likely to be opened and read. E-mail also allows you to nurture a relationship with the audience, but along with that necessitates that you personalize or customize your messages for optimal relevancy. Keep in mind, consumers receive many e-mails in a day, and there is a high probability your e-mail may be deleted without even being opened. Therefore, the idea of a consumer having opted into your e-mail is important (as this shows interest in your offerings) as well as effective use of the subject line. In fact, almost 16 percent of all e-mails never actually make it into the inbox (E-mail Tool Tester 2019), which shows how spam filters can also impact your e-mailing strategy.

Regardless of technological advances and the plethora of social platforms that now exist, e-mail is still one of the best ways to present an offer to a prospective consumer or existing consumer. The content created for social media platforms, as mentioned in Chapter 3, can be repurposed for e-mail. Likewise, content created such as a podcast can be repurposed for e-mail as can a blog post. Utilizing the same and similar content between platforms creates continuity and reinforces a brand message. By now, you should be seeing this as a recurrent theme throughout the book. It is essential that you create and nurture this brand identity and message in a thoughtful and cohesive way.

Unfortunately, the notion of e-mail marketing has long been associated with being untrustworthy and unsolicited. In the past, we saw misuse of information and bombarding consumers with e-mails they had no way of opting out of. Over time, e-mail marketing has seen some changes that have provided consumers ways to opt out of communications or to easily opt into only specific brand communications while still facilitating the communication between brand and consumer. Spam e-mail still is an issue for many, on average Spam e-mails account for approximately 54 percent of all e-mail traffic, down from 71 percent in April of 2014 (Statista 2020b). Even with all of the negative associations consumers have with e-mail, it is still considered one of the most effective marketing activities for brand building, improving relationships, gaining new contacts, and promoting sales for a company.

Cross Channel Touch Points

We have been discussing channels in the context of communicating with consumers, however, the same digital channels are also responsible and the delivery of products and services. Retailers, for example, are experiencing a dramatic shift in the buying habits of consumers and face similar integration challenges with on and offline channels in order to sustain a competitive advantage (Mark et al. 2019). There has been an increase in the number of customers who shop online rather in brick and mortar locations. Worth noting are the dramatic changes in business models many businesses were forced to make in 2020, including retail, that became necessary due to the Coronavirus Pandemic. New types of retail channels and touchpoints have emerged over the past decade to influence consumer behavior, even prior to the Pandemic.

The idea of multichannel retailing has become common due to the inevitable preferences for digital channels over more traditional ones (Kannan and Li 2017). Online retailers are recognizing the value of mobile and the influx of m-commerce, the process of making purchases via mobile. Consumers are shopping from their smartphones and tablets, with the number of smart phone users reaching an estimated 3.5 billion users (Statista 2020a). The concept of buying online but picking up in person at a store, known as BOPIS, is now considered to be one of the most valuable arenas of the retail shopping experience. COVID-19 and associated societal changes, really boosted this offering by many businesses, and forced others to join big-box retailers like Target and Walmart to leverage BOPIS. Buying online and picking up in store (BOPIS) offers many benefits for both customers and retailer, while also allowing for more personalized and meaningful experiences. Personalization simply means providing a customer experience that is well aligned with consumer preferences and needs; personalization helps organizations be relevant to existing and potential customers (Kolekar et al. 2018). As we see this offering evolve, AI-powered personalization engines will support BOPIS, and become a valuable tool when further integrated into customer engagement analytics by shaping the future of online engagement. The use of mobile channels, specifically smartphones, has revolutionized the shopping experience (Hickman et al. 2020), and contributed to the focus on both online consumer behavior and omnichannel approaches that enhance the consumer shopping experience.

Often in the realm of retail, channels are managed and accounted for separately resulting in lack of integration of the channels. It has become a challenge for many retailers to integrate channels and strategies, thus creating varying customer experiences. Many channels are now somewhat interchangeable, so customers are using multiple channels, thus providing consistent and seamless customer experience has never been more important. Businesses should aim to adopt a more holistic mindset that focuses on the influencing of the process rather than focusing only on the consumer decision outcome (Faulds et al. 2018) and the traditional transactional mindset. Knowledge of a consumer such as demographic and socioeconomic data, past purchases, and shared purchase intentions allows retailers to truly understand situational relevance of a shopping encounter and be able to add value to the shopping journey (Faulds et al. 2018).

Most retailers offer mobile shopping apps, and it is not uncommon for a consumer to be comparing products on and offline, between retailers, and the arriving at making a final purchase via mobile due to the streamlined user experience and ability to shop at any time, and anywhere. There is also an increase in the number of discounts offered and in the variety of ways they are offered. Followers of a brand on Instagram may be privy to a flash sale, or e-mail subscribers may get a weekend coupon code. This allows for the individualization of the shopping journey for participates across all stages of the purchase process. Those businesses who are successful, have adopted a concierge approach to really embrace a relevant experience that consumers demand. For example, grocery retailer Kroger offers an App that allows the consumer to create and maintain a shopping list, clip digital coupons, while offering in-store navigation tools, and also allowing for convenient in person pickup. Starbucks, as we mentioned earlier in our readings about mobile, offers multiple capabilities via their mobile app. Their loyalty program is one of the key feature's users enjoy, as well as the ability to order and pick up. The key to their success with the app is their ability to leverage digital engagement. Starbucks does this so seamlessly in a way that is not overbearing to the user. The app offers the ability to order and to pay ahead of time, and even facilitates locating where the closest Starbucks location is, along with the menu and the ability to place an order at that particular location. The app also includes featured food and beverages, keeping the users informed about new products, while differentiating it from the competition. Home Depot is merging both the physical and digital world to offer a robust interconnected experience. Users are able to shop both online and in person, with features that help consumers find products within the store as well as inventory amounts. The app also includes an augmented reality feature, showing the 360-degree product view with video buying guides. And of course, Amazon. The Amazon app clearly mimics their online retailing site and has become one of the most used apps for consumers. Not only do consumers use Amazon for everyday purchases, they are using it as a price comparison tool when shopping on other websites and at brick and mortar retailers. All of these examples highlight the convenience mobile applications bring to the consumer as well as how they enhance their sense of empowerment. As marketers, you cannot design touch points in isolation, the consumer of today uses a very wide range of touchpoints as part of both on, and offline experiences. It is important to shift from an approach focusing on each individual touch point, and instead design for the entire experience in order to provide value throughout the customer journey.

Key Takeaways

This idea of a connected consumer, created by the smart phone (or other mobile device), has pushed marketers to think outside of the box. No longer is the location for a purchase the focus. Consumers now expect to be able to access information and purchasing options 24/7, making the idea of an integrated omnichannel a paramount initiative for markets to improve the customer experience across all channels. The growth of the number of tech savvy consumers coupled with the growth of mobile use and prevalence of internet connections, has essentially contributed to the evolution of ecommerce and the associated marketing strategies.

We have seen advances in mobile marketing over the past decade. Several trends persist, and new ones are on the horizon. Geolocation is such a trend that has made a significant impact to many industries in that advertisers are able to target more effectively. Similarly, mobile commerce or m-commerce is making an impact in many industries given the multitude of new ways consumers are able to pay for products and services, with more applications yet to come. Mobile, and the empowerment it delivers, is supporting a shift in customer relationships from transactional based to value based, creating somewhat sustainable brand loyalty by way of delivering relevant experiences that consumers now demand. Through a strategic approach, mobile offers marketers a way to seamlessly connect digital channels, impact the user experience, and facilitate more meaningful encounters.

E-mail access by mobile phone has become commonplace and plays a large part in a successful digital strategy. In order to have a successful e-mail marketing campaign, it is imperative to first establish explicit objectives and tie them to the appropriate metrics. Correctly defining the desired results ensures the ability to measure the effectiveness and success of the e-mail campaign and associated marketing activities (Hudák, et al. 2017). Most marketers utilized e-mail as a way to create personal experiences, including personalized offers. However, an effective e-mail strategy is coordinated with your other channels, as we have been uncovering through this book. E-mail must also represent your brand appropriately and speak to the narrative you have established for your organization while also attempting to guide consumers through the buyer's journey: awareness, consideration, conversion, loyalty, and then advocacy. As marketers, we should be taking advantage of this unique opportunity to leverage the one to one connection that e-mail and mobile can provide.

CHAPTER 5

Data Driven Decision Making

Learning Objectives

- Identify key performance indicator (KPI) data for supporting recommendations regarding future digital marketing decisions.
- Understand how strategic use of analytics can inform an integrated digital strategy.
- Recognize the many ways to utilize data effectively to generate valuable and actionable managerial insights for informed decision making.

As we have seen, digital marketing encompasses a lot of various platforms and tools. All of the elements of a digital marketing strategy should be measured. Collecting data is important, but simply aggregating that data is not enough. Brands need to understand how to analyze the data, understand what the data is "saying", and then translate this information to address business objectives. There are now massive amounts of data available through digital platforms and tools. This coupled with newer and innovative analysis capabilities, have led to a deeper understanding of consumer behavior as well as a more accurate view of the effectiveness of marketing and business strategies. A primary advantage of digital versus traditional marketing efforts is that digital can provide a much clearer image of results, and in a much faster timeframe. Unfortunately, many new digital marketers may not fully understand the data or know exactly how to best utilize it. Often too, there will be confusion as to what should be measured in the first place.

The more data driven your business is, the higher your return on investment will be. Data-driven marketing decisions are made possible through the abundance of metrics digital analytics and digital platforms allow. Metrics are specific measures that allow marketers to compare results in relation to specific marketing objectives, they are used to track the status of a specific business process. Without metrics, we are unable to truly know the effectiveness of our digital efforts. Different metrics are more valuable for different areas of business, and the varying decisions made therein. Key performance indicators (KPIs), on the other hand, are measurable values that show you just how effective efforts are at achieving business objectives. KPIs determine a hit or miss, whereas a metrics simply tracks progress and can be considered data points. For example, a common marketing metric is tracking SEO keyword rankings. It is not necessarily a marketing KPI as it is not a direct link to business objective. Each KPI can be considered a metric, but not every metric can be considered a KPI. It is not uncommon for businesses to have KPI for each channel, with metrics influencing the KPIs.

Key performance indicators are directly tied to how your organization makes money. Therefore, organizations must develop a clear and integrated digital marketing strategy, aligned with organization goals and accurate key performance indicators. Organizations that do not have a strategy defined and in place, will encounter significant issues in measuring success. The lack of a clear strategy and defined goals leads to choosing irrelevant KPIs and inaccurate measures of success that will ultimately lead an organization down the wrong path, and success will become illusive.

Analytics

Accurate information is a key success factor in the performance of decision makers. Leaders and decision makers are able to gain valuable insights from the multiple data sources that digital provides. Big data analytics enhance and support decision making within an organization by integrating data analytics into decision making processes. Big data simply refers to the large volume of data the businesses have access to, and analytics relates to providing operational insight for a business. Consider big data to be a large collection of information, whereas analytics to be specific information that you review to find answers to business questions. Digital marketing involves a lot of data and embraces the practice of analytics. There are multiple opportunities to gather analytics for various digital initiatives that are available to both large and smaller businesses. In this age of data and information overload, marketers from all segments of industry need to understand what this means for their business. The ability to make smart data driven decisions is key!

At the heart of every digital campaign is the website. As we explored earlier, the website can be used for multiple purposes, to include contact information, relevant content, and more. Data collection from your website has been simplified significantly due to Google Analytics. Google Analytics is a tool that gathers data from a website to help inform your digital marketing decisions. Google Analytics tracks visitors from search engines, provides data to show what is going on within your website, offers information on your audience such as demographics and interests, offers information on how your users arrived at your website, offers information on what people do when they are on your website such as how long they stay on the page, and also provides information related to subscribing or purchasing. Google Analytics also provides an overview of your page views and the time spent on the website, as well as number of conversions, bounce rate, and even revenue generated by e-mail campaign.

If you are a beginner, you should at least be measuring bounce rate, conversion rate, and channels on Google Analytics. A bounce is when a visitor enters your page, but then leaves without doing anything else. A conversion is the number of visitors who turn into lead after doing a specific action on the webpage, such as sign up for your blog or newsletter. Finally, channels simply show where the visitors are coming from. If you see your bounce rate is high, you would want to take a look as to why the visitors do not click or navigate on the site. This is a key indicator of poor user experience. If your leads are high, you deserve a pat on the back. High traffic to your site is good, but it means little if visitors take no action and thus do not convert to leads. When looking at the various digital channels, you will be able to see what sites your visitors are coming from. Are they coming from a link you embedded in a Tweet on Twitter? Are they navigating to your site from a link from another brand? Or are they finding their way to your site from a paid digital ad? You will also be able to see just how much of your traffic comes from social, SEO, paid, and referrals to better inform your strategy moving forward.

There are a variety of tools for analytics other than Google Analytics, such as StatCounter, Clicky, Canecto, Matomo, and Kissmetrics. Google Analytics and Kissmetrics are essential tools for your digital marketing toolbelt. Understanding where the traffic is coming from can inform many marketing decisions. Consider some customer find their way to your website via e-mail; search through Google; advertisement on Google or Facebook; link on a nonbranded blog, forum or social media post. Visits could also stem from your own social media channels with links to your website, and folks simply typing in your website address or utilizing a bookmark. Armed with this type of information, a brand has better optics into how consumers find their way to a particular website and what channels are most effective and least effective. Recall, in previous chapters, we spoke about how search engine marketing and search engine optimization can drive a visitor to your website, as well as how social media and digital advertising can drive a visitor to your website.

Knowing what is pulling consumers to your website will help you further leverage that particular tool. For example, should your brand notice significant traffic originating from a particular link in a branded blog post, this could indicate the particular article resonated with your audience, along with that particular link and its content. Consider a brand advocate sharing an image of your product in a social media post with a link to your website. Or possibly a brand advocate with a blog post mentioning your product with a link to your page. Also consider the possibility of looking at your audience and identifying demographic or psychographic data that may differ from what you have aligned to your brand or product. This could indicate an opportunity that may have been overlooked. Knowing this information not only helps inform future strategic decisions, but can also identify strengths and opportunities for your existing campaign.

Google Analytics offers the user the ability to create custom reporting for your digital marketing initiatives. While Google Analytics does not allow you to track data back to any type of personal identifiable information, it does allow you to track data related to a particular device, location in the world, and pages they have visited. However, no information such as a name or e-mail address is offered. Google offers a tremendous amount of information on their website to include videos and coursework related to the tool. Understanding how Google Analytics works, and the information that it can provide is a key component to a digital marketing strategy. Recall, your goals and objectives of the digital marketing strategy must tie back to business objectives. Likewise, these digital marketing goals and objectives must be measurable. In the onset of your strategizing, identifying these objectives and related measurement opportunities will be one of the first things you do. An obvious strength of a digital marketing campaign is the ability to review data in real time throughout the length of a campaign rather than awaiting the end of the campaign and reflecting back with data in hand. Also be wary of tracking the wrong metrics. The components of a digital marketing campaign are highly trackable, and it can be possible to be using Google Analytics and be tracking the wrong metrics.

Understanding Users and Platforms

It is important to understand that viewing metrics in isolation of each other fails to offer a complete picture of your users' behaviors. Qualitative data is also important to a campaign. Whereas look at numerical data or quantitative data, the qualitative data is more easily observed but not measured. Think of your user's behavior. Qualitative data is extremely helpful in combination with the quantitative data. Qualitative data gathering involves tracking clicks, or mouse movement, scrolling, a visual representation of this interaction with your website is called a heat map. You can also find a lot of qualitative information simply by engaging with your audience on these digital channels. While creating goals and objectives and sitting up reporting in Google Analytics to measure all of your hard work is important, never underestimate the value of engaging with customers. Not only does it contribute to your branding efforts and loyalty, it also offers a wealth of information in regard to return on investment and qualitative data. Much like in a real life relationship, the digital marketer's relationship with consumers is one that may take time to build, nurture, and leverage. Consider the efforts in your digital marketing strategy as steps in a relationship, hopefully culminating with a sale after a relationship has been established and nurtured, and is reciprocal in nature.

Analytics are the key to understanding users and are quite essential to a company's growth, regardless of the digital platform. Without analytics, you won't be able to identify the most appropriate ways to spend marketing resources and dollars. Measuring social media efforts with analytics ensures you focus time, effort, and budget on channels and tactics that are shown to be effective. Regularly tracking and reporting on established metrics will allow you to pivot your strategy if and as needed. Social media analytics will illuminate which content is working on your social platforms, allowing you to leverage content that resonates with an audience on a specific social platform. Mobile also offers significant amounts of valuable and actional data. With this information, you will be better able to optimize your mobile application and strategy for growth, performance, and customer satisfaction. Within mobile analytics, you will want to define every step within the customer journey. This journey will map out how a user is guided from downloading the application all the way to purchase and will inform a significant portion of your mobile strategy while offering optics into the user experience. Understanding organizational goals will help to identify and understand which metrics matter and provide critical insight for your organization. Knowing who your users are and what they are doing within your app answers our key questions for mobile analytics. Analytics for e-mail ensures your understanding of how e-mail is supporting goal achievement. Your e-mail marketing goals may be different from the goals of other organizations, or they might very within your organization over time. Therefore, it's important to be diligent about which e-mail metrics you will be tracking and ensure you are able to effectively and accurately measure e-mail performance and alignment with the overarching goals.

Social media offers many free and paid analytics tools. For example, Hootsuite Analytics, Brandwatch, Facebook Analytics, Twitter Analytics, Instagram Insights, Pinterest Analytics, and of course Google Analytics. As you can see, most of the social media management platforms include a built-in analytics tool to help save the user time and make it easier to compare results across networks. Google Analytics is primarily for website information, but you can use it to also set up reports that can help provide insight into which social media platforms provide the most traffic, what content seems to work best on what social network, look at leads and conversions coming from social media, and help calculate return on investment (ROI) of a social media campaign.

Return on investment (ROI) is the measure of profitability (Tuten and Soloman 2018). In an effort to determine the most accurate ROI, we look at the financial value of the resources used to execute a strategy, measure the financial outcomes, and then calculate the ratio between the inputs and outcomes. Regardless of the digital platform or tools used within additional marketing campaign, revenue is a primary focus for any organization. ROI is an essential metric for any business trying to determine the impact of its digital marketing activities. With all the data digital provides, many organizations still underutilize the analytics in regard to digital marketing. The idea of data driven marketing to ensure individualization of marketing messages is not fully leveraged by many organizations. Data collecting tools, like Google Analytics, allow users to track the return on investment of a campaign through a variety of lenses. Seeing what is working and what is not working allows for you to make changes in your approach in a very agile way.

ROI begins with establishing SMART goals that are specific, measurable, achievable, relevant, and timely. Unlike setting business goals, ROI goals become difficult to determine. Metrics tend to be somewhat overvalued specifically when speaking of social media. It's easy to measure the likes, shares, and comments on Facebook, however, they do not have a direct impact on revenue. Social media functions exceed ROI (Mahoney and Tang 2017). In some instances, it is difficult to align a financial value to social media inputs and outcomes. For example, what is the value of a social media like or share? How does that change with the influence of one user over another? Does this fluctuate over time? How might one tie a piece of user generated content on Twitter to the brand loyalty of segments of the population? How do we connect a like with a purchase? However, likes shares and comments can improve a brand's ranking in search through Google and other search engines. Thus, they are not entirely void of value. Social media has moved away from purely focusing solely on the quantitative assessment of campaigns. Consider the use of both qualitative and quantitative methodologies to understand how your audience reacts to social media initiatives. Looking at the impact from a more consumer centric lens will allow you to really understand how social media can be leveraged at each stage of the customer journey as well as each stage of your campaign. Not only do you want to measure the engagement on social platforms with consumers, but you will also want to investigate how all the utilized digital platforms interact with one another.

Key Takeaways

An advantage of the digital landscape is that it becomes much easier to acquire data on specific customer touchpoints; this data is useful for measuring the efficiency and effectiveness of various marketing initiatives thereby optimizing the marketing dollar (Kannan and Li 2017). Not every digital marketing campaign leads to dollars. Some campaigns may be tied to creating or improving brand awareness, while others may simply just be to bring visitors to your website. Both may help improve profits in the long run, however, short-term results will not be aligned to monetary value. It's important to understand the why behind the data and undercovering motivations of your customers, and this becomes possible through both quantitative data and qualitative data. Reviewing and understanding the various data analytics within a digital campaign allows marketers to see the impacts of digital initiatives more holistically.

Digital affords marketers the ability to adjust or abandoned campaigns that are not working in real time. Utilizing analytics to gather and interpret data and monitor digital trends enables an organization to plan better opportunities and make better marketing decisions. Analytics provide actionable insights that can be leveraged to further engage users, attract and retain customers, and ultimately impact ROI.

CHAPTER 6

The Synergistic Relationship

Learning Objectives

- Analyze strategic use of branding as part of a digital strategy.
- Understand the impact of technology on the future of digital marketing.
- Understand how a brand can ensure authenticity through a cohesive message.

David Ogilvy, considered to be the "Father of Advertising," once said many years ago: "a brand is the consumer's idea of a product" (Blackston 2000). As this quote captures, the consumer is an active participant in the creation of brand equity. As marketers, if we want to understand and manage the intangibles such as brand equity directly, we need to look at the consumer as an associated brand relationship. A brand relationship is an extension of the notion of brand personality, and it is the building block of long-term relevancy and success.

As we have seen, infusing traditional marketing with digital tools is an in depth and ongoing process. Digital marketing spans all the areas of a business and must be done strategically with the end consumer in mind, with identifying the most appropriate channels for a specific campaign, and aligning business objectives with digital marketing campaigns. Digital marketers are tasked with ensuring a digital experience that offers quality, privacy, and security, while also supporting the buying process and continuing to develop lifetime customer relationships. Consumers move through the buying process through various stages of awareness, familiarity, consideration, evaluation, purchase, and post purchase evaluation. If consumers are receiving value throughout this process, they are likely to become loyal customers and move through the decision journey in a fundamentally new way (Kannan and Li 2017). This journey will often span both the digital and landscape and offline environments. Strategic and integrated digital marketing that is both effective and efficient can be a source of organizational strength (Aaker 2015). Nonetheless, many organizations still struggle to fully leverage and apply digital in a way that truly captures the synergistic power of digital.

Digital technologies and platforms are still considered new in contrast to our traditional methods and platforms. This provides opportunities for digital disruptors to adapt and leverage the changes to the landscape. Such disruptors have changed the landscape and become leaders in various industries, think of Amazon and its journey as well as Uber, AirBnB, and Netflix. These brands have impacted both consumer expectations and consumer behaviors in our culture, in many markets and industries, and have driven many technological advances. However, the transformation to a digital business is not easy, it takes a lot of planning, organizational capabilities, and integration of digital channels into existing marketing initiatives. While digital marketing plans address customer acquisition and retention using 'digital' tools and platforms, the plan must also fully support overall business goals as outlined within the organization business plans. An effective digital marketing plan will span across an organization's varying functions, and also be part of a larger cohesive marketing plan.

There are constant changes within the realm of digital marketing impacting social media, search engine optimization, pay per click, content marketing, and more. This will result in the landscape evolving over time. We see significant shifts within the field already, and these changes should not be ignored. Organizations must accept the influence of the digital landscape. It is imperative for marketers to do the research and explore digital possibilities to understand the most effective platforms and strategies to embrace. Digital technologies are forever changing the environment within which business operates, and consumer behavior is also changing as a result of these technologies (Kannan and Li 2017). Throughout this text, we have covered various areas of digital marketing, and how they relate to one another in the context of branding and engagement. An effective digital strategy will help to build relationships through interactions and communications, while also engaging the customer in cocreation of value. In the past, value creation was understood to be solely the job of the organization, but with the significance of consumer centric and service dominant perspectives, the idea of value creation has evolved.

Communicating a Cohesive Marketing Message

The number of touchpoints marketers now have with consumers along their journey leads to a strong increase in market coverage for a brand. This also means a more complex strategy is needed to make the experience seamless and balanced. Integrated-marketing communication (IMC) becomes increasingly difficult in the digital landscape. Marketing managers need to have a very adaptive mindset along with the willingness to continuously engage in learning, and drive the process of implementing unique and value creating content that takes into account broader integrated marketing communications and associated initiatives (Hollebeek and Macky 2019). Brands must choose from a variety of methods to include mobile, social, digital advertising, e-mail, and more. Organizations use these various types of digital media to convey the same kinds of marketing messages. However, the message may vary dependent on the organization and medium, and there are times when these varying techniques may compete with each other. Resulting in efforts that do not reinforce the brand as intended. Consider the challenges presented with integrating both online and offline communication. It is a complex landscape requiring a strategic yet agile approach. Customers should be at the center of all the initiatives, as they are in control. It is somewhat easy to deliver customized content to consumers, but it is extremely challenging to do so across all the digital channels, while also taking into account the existing offline communications.

Online or digital communication mediums facilitate two-way communications and interactions that brands can, and should, leverage to build relationships with consumers. Every interaction between a consumer and a brand serves to build relationships. When we embrace the idea of relationship marketing through these digital channels, the customer and the brand work together collaboratively to meet shared goals through digital communication, feedback, and engagement. The profitability of both building and sustaining long-term relationships between consumers and brands is well documented through the literature surrounding marketing.

A top reason why many organizations fail to capture and harness digital in a synergistic way is due to the tendency to view digital as a stand-alone activity, with many specific tools therein. However, this is a rather simplistic way to view the landscape. Successful digital implementation takes a keen understanding of not only the various platforms and tools, but also the understanding of varying specific objectives, players, and metrics and how they can be combined in many different ways to create distinctly different types of strategies. In order to be effective, a digital strategy must be fully customized or tailored to a business objective. Most often, we look at digital as a way to simply support an offering, focusing on ways to make an offering more understandable and credible, and making the purchase process easier (Aaker 2015). However, there are many other ways digital is used to contribute to the brand and business, and what works for one business and its goals and market position will vary with another.

The different elements of digital can help support and amplify brand-building initiatives, and they work synergistically to support and reinforce each other. As we revisit our earlier example of searching for "shoes for high arches," a social media post on Facebook or Instagram can support and reinforce messages from the website while also driving traffic to the site. Similarly, e-mail newsletters can support the web content and drive traffic to the site, and a mobile app could facilitate and support the shopping experience. Alternatively, a website or blog could drive curious consumers to social feeds to see what is being shared by the brand, and they may then be able to engage more with the brand via the social platforms.

A strategic digital marketing plan will significantly impact an organization's position, resources, and management over time (Acker 2015). It is quite important that there be an experienced senior marketer involved at every stage of the strategic planning. The role of digital within an organization is absolutely not of a standalone team, no matter how good the people on the team are. It is imperative to include some form of cross functional team communication through planning, implementing, and measuring.

Current Industry Trends Surrounding Digital Marketing

As you are planning a digital initiative, have you done a competitive analysis? What are your competitors doing on the various digital platforms?

What type of content is on their websites? What type of content is on their social media? What keywords are working for the competition? What do customers say about the competition? Understanding where you are within the digital landscape in respect to the competition and aspirant brands, can help inform parts of a digital campaign.

As technology advances and the digital landscape evolves, trends within the industry will also evolve. At this time, we are seeing an increase in shoppable posts via Instagram and Facebook, facilitating the shopping experience while also harnessing the power of influencer marketing and peer to peer communications. Content marketing is also continuing to be leveraged in many different ways, including storytelling, and will continue to be an integral part of all areas of the digital landscape to leverage. Technology is pushing virtual and augmented reality (VR and AR) into the digital landscape. Imagine a branded experience by way of a VR headset. A customer is able to visualize how a product may look in their home, or even tour remote facilities. Making more interactive experiences through AR and VR can enhance and strengthen connections with consumers. Chatbots are becoming more common on websites to facilitate customer service inquiries as well as guiding a user on a website to improve customer experience. We will see more artificial intelligence informing these chatbots in the future. Digital technologies and platforms that we have covered throughout this text, along with artificial intelligence and deep learning, all show significant promise in the transformation of the lives of consumers (Kannan and Li 2017). It will be interesting to see how the developments in the landscape will also reshape marketing.

As consumers become inundated with marketing messages on nearly every platform and channel, it becomes increasingly important to develop programs and initiatives that resonate with the consumer. We see this within video and viral shares, supporting the notion that relevant content is still paramount. User generated content (UGC) will continue to be a popular trend. Domino's Pizza leveraged UGC more than a decade ago with an initiative where consumers submitted home videos to be leveraged for Domino's environmentally friendly recycling campaign. Brands continue to utilize the user generated content as content generated by the end user can become an extremely powerful marketing tool. This was an especially popular technique more recently during COVID-19 when many consumers were isolated at home. Consumers began creating content via video that was soon scooped up by brands in the form of commercials and even supporting an entire weekly television show. For example, CBS broadcast an entire TV show leveraging consumer video. The Greatest #StayAtHome Videos Began airing that May with actor and stand-up comedian Cedric the Entertainer hosting. The show ran some of the best videos people had made while staying in quarantine, with added commentary on those videos. While many videos were funny, a common theme was how viewers could identify with the frustrations of staying home for extended periods of time.

Consider some of the "feel good" campaigns we have seen over the years via social media and other online and offline media. Many brands have leveraged this approach and really explored ways in which campaigns could resonate with consumers as well as take a more positive approach. Creating inspirational campaigns that appeal to our emotions, and the good of humanity will always be on trend. We see this a lot during the holiday season, where online and offline marketing materials tap into our emotional sides. This is often done by making connections for the viewer between the brand and positive feelings, emotions, or motivations. This is typically done through storytelling, a popular and effective tool for marketers. Storytelling can be an effective way to invigorate your brand.

Storytelling is closely tied to the idea of content marketing by allowing you to give products and services an identity by telling a story through content. Remember, a brand is a matter of perception, and when you tell a story that embraces the human element, you create an experience that can resonate with your customers. Stories are an essential form of our communication as humans, and it is often one of the first ways we share norms and values. Research has shown that the human brain encodes information, stores information, and retrieves information in a narrative form. Just as stories are passed generation to generation, we still tell stories but in a more digital way through new media. It is a common practice in blog writing, as we read in Chapter 3, and this notion of a good story applies to branding and digital marketing as well. Traditional elements of storytelling apply in the digital space: a good story has an interesting plot, and characters that audiences can identify with. The plot should evoke feelings and emotions that pull the audience in and capture their attention.

One way for brands to ensure authenticity of their brand and brand messages is the use of storytelling (Mahoney and Tang 2017). Stories offer marketers the ability to deliver important information and shape decisions as well as the overall brand experience. The notion of storytelling is a key strategy in digital marketing as it will continue to be a key differentiator among brands. We see various levels of storytelling within video marketing strategies, social media strategies, mobile strategies, and more (Romo et al. 2017). Storytelling can contribute to brand awareness, consumer interaction, and motivations for purchase. The variety of digital technologies, platforms, and players make it possible to pull an audience into the story, where they become a part of that story and part of the communication of that story.

It becomes important for traditional marketers to understand why consumers engage in storytelling and how to leverage the role of consumer generated content within a brand story (Gosline et al. 2017). Thus, marketing in the context of research, could be considered a function that is part social scientist and part storyteller (Cluley et al. 2020). Meaning, marketers utilize digital channels to not only collect and analyze data, but they are also reporting findings in ways that can contribute to the narrative. Marketers are also immersed in the experiences of the consumer; they understand the data and are able to communicate the data in ways that inform engagement strategy objectives, decision, and KPIs. The second role being one of a "story-teller," utilizing the findings to truly bring the customer to life and inform decisions related to producing a story for narrative that resonates with the audience. This brings to light the division between qualitative and quantitative data, forcing marketing to embrace both ideals to create and maintain a narrative that is not only valuable, but strategic. Brands should engage consumers to generate believable yet compelling stories.

Gosline et al. (2017) found that consumer-based storytelling does in fact influence people to consider purchases. On average, there was an increase of 32 percent in purchasing considerations when story telling was utilized. The authors also found that people who were exposed to brand stories had significantly higher connection and trust in those brands. Therefore, serious consideration should be made by brands who are not strategically contributing to the narrative with a goal of including consumers in the story. When considering a strategic approach to utilize storytelling within your digital strategy, content will be a significant part of an effective campaign. As content is created for the story, you should look to the target audience as well as the sales funnel to ensure the content is not only interesting and engaging, but also persuades and effectively communicates the intended message to the target audience, Keep in mind, this content should not only resonate with your audience, but also be entertaining, functional, and informative (Aaker 2015). Content can help add depth to your brands digital story regardless if it is from the brands perspective, or the consumers perspective through user generated content.

The strategic use of keywords within your content allows it to be discoverable, much like other digital initiatives we have explored through this book. Once content is created or curated, you must still actively promote it. The internet, mobile devices, social platforms, and the like facilitate the promotion of storytelling content to contribute to the digital narrative. Leveraging the appropriate channels will help you to connect with the intended audience and drive website traffic, as well as improve engagement and help to inform a buyer's purchasing decision. Do not focus on quantity over quality. On all the platforms and tools we have discussed thus far, quality trumps quantity. Simply posting multiple times per day on social media does not automatically guarantee clicks and traffic to your website, nor does prolific blogging.

If you offer nothing of value, and content does a little to improve someone's life, you will have wasted your time. Being strategic in your approach to content is absolutely paramount. What problem can you solve? How does your brand help? What do typical questions folks ask related to your business? Story telling has been a central way for societies to convey attitudes and values, and it will remain a key source of information and influence within a digital landscape (Gosline et al. 2017). The importance of a well thought out and strategic approach to content creation and curation cannot be understated. As new technologies like VR evolve and improve, we will see new opportunities to use consumer storytelling within digital strategies (Gosline et al. 2017).

Key Takeaways

A brand encompasses all the tangible and intangible characteristics of an organization, such as logo, name, product, employees, the environment such as brick and mortar stores, website, its social networks, and even reputation and perceptions. As we look at the strategic approaches to branding, it is important to establish clear and distinctive identities for products, services, and the organization as well.

Aligning your marketing goals with sales goals clearly can also be difficult and a roadblock for some. Often sales and marketing do not realize they serve very different purposes but are on the same team with the same goal. In order to achieve this goal of a satisfied customer, marketing folks work to harness brand awareness and identify prospects and leads whereas sales teams focus on closing those leads. If the customer experience from point A to point B was less than awesome, no one has reached their goal. The customer is the center of every objective of your business. Marketing has evolved to result in catering more to the customer than ever before.

With a well-planned digital approach, businesses are better able to meet these varying consumer needs while also enjoying higher profits. Engaging consumer-centric marketing is an ongoing process that should be infused at each step of any strategic initiative as well as infused at every level of your organization. It may be that you need to rethink your organizations business model, or even adjust your core values. Often brands will be distracted by the newest tool or tactic. While some of these new tools and tactics have shown to be effective and of value, more often than not your best bet would be to concentrate on what has been working for you thus far.

Within the digital environment, there is a plethora of information that is demanding the attention of consumers. Your challenge as marketers is not only related to creation of valuable content, but also about getting the attention of your intended audience as well. Integration can be difficult; it requires an organization to function in all the areas as a team. The utilization of big data across channels is key, but so is having the right players to staff the organization. Folks who understand how to clean, organize, and integrate data will be called upon and relied upon, just as folks who can translate these numbers into language the c-suite can understand. Retention of these key individuals brings many areas of an organization to the table with a call to action. Technology cannot be ignored, it too is a major player in the way we can integrate all the channels, being aware of new technologies as well as how they can be leveraged strategically and efficiently is paramount.

Closing Thoughts

Challenges, Changes, and Shifts

Technology has advanced significantly since the 20th century, and now, we are quite likely on the cusp of the fourth industrial revolution that will impact all areas of our lives, including business. Whereas we saw steam in the first industrial revolution, electricity in the second, silicon in the third, we will see digital technology and data entwined in everything during this fourth industrial revolution.

In this digital age, with the customer at the helm, marketers have their work cut out for them. Building brands in this digital era with distracted and empowered customers, necessitates a shift from company centric brand management to one that is more customer obsessed and one that creates an exceptional and resonant brand experience. It is imperative to recognize how the role of marketers is evolving in the digital age, and the importance of data driven decisions. As we have seen, many businesses are reorganizing and embedding marketing research and associated strategies to leverage and harness the power of digital platforms and technologies. The ways in which we study consumer behavior and perform marketing research must incorporate digital technology. However, we find that marketers often lack the technical skills and support from the overall organization to really take advantage of digital technologies.

Marketing thought leaders are shifting focus on developing the technical skills needed in the landscape. This combination of being a marketing expert who also encompass some technical skills associated with digital will become a prerequisite for employment within the field. For example, a marketing professional who also has a solid understanding of Google Analytics is highly desirable. Not to mention a marketing professional who understands the concepts of inbound marketing and the importance of content throughout. It is becoming more and more important for my fellow marketers to push themselves to acquire new skills within digital. It is recommended that marketing professionals become lifelong learners if they are not already. Part of the inspiration for this book are my marketing students who realize the importance a higher education and lifelong learning. My students show grit, determination, and the desire to learn. As we watch technology advance, it has become important for my students to differentiate themselves with the skills they either need for the workplace, have a passion for, or simply need support in. It has always been my suggestion for students to pursue industry recognized credentials to further support their growth and value for employers.

There are many certifications that will add value to the employee and to the organization. Some suggested courses and credentials are mentioned in the following list, some are free. Note that some may evolve over time or change course or credential name:

- Facebook BluePrint Certification: Facebook Certified Digital Marketing Associate
- Facebook BluePrint Certification: Facebook Certified Marketing Science Professional
- Hubspot's Content Marketing Certificate
- Hubspot's Social Media Marketing Certificate
- Hubspot's Inbound Marketing Certificate
- Hubspot's Content Marketing Certificate
- Hubspot's Email Marketing Certificate
- Hubspot's Contextual Marketing Certificate
- Hootsuite Platform Certification
- Hootsuite Social Marketing Certification
- Snapchat Advertising Core Competencies Certification
- Google Analytics IQ Certification
- Google Ads Certification
- Google Search Engine Optimization Fundamentals Certificate
- Amazon Sponsored Ads Accreditation Certification
- Bing Ads Certification
- YouTube Creator Academy Certification
- Institute for Brand Marketing: Advanced Marketing Technologies
- Institute for Brand Marketing: Monetizing Engagement Badge

- Digital Marketing Institute: Certified Digital Marketing Professional
- LinkedIn Learning Lead Generation with Social Media Course
- Yoast SEO Academy
- Twitter Flight School

There will undoubtedly be more challenges, changes, and shifts in the landscape of digital and marketing, as well as the expectations of consumers. Being open minded and staying abreast of trends and challenges will serve a marketer well. The key is to consider the user experience along all digital platforms, how can you make it a truly excellent, personalized experience? Personalization will become key as we see more brands deliver on digital platforms and more technologies facilitate this process. Personalization will be achieved by utilizing the various data available affectively, and targeting consumers based on that particular data. However, there are many challenges associated with personalization including costs, data privacy issues and laws, and the security of the personal data collected. We will see future trends surrounding personalization using machine learning and artificial intelligence in order to target users in real time with relevant advertising. Knowing who your customers are is becoming increasingly important and will inevitably be what determines the success of your marketing strategies, digital or otherwise.

Stay in touch via my social channels and let me know how you are changing the landscape of Digital Marketing ~ JR

https://twitter.com/drjrogers or @drjrogers
https://www.linkedin.com/in/jessica-rogers-smm/

References

Aaker, D. 1996. *Building Strong Brands*. New York, NY: n.p.

Aaker, D. 2015. *Four Ways Digital Works to Build Brands and Relationships*, 37–37. http://henrystewartpublications.com/jbs

Aaker, D., and A. Marcum. 2017. "The Satisfied vs. Committed Brand Loyalist and What Drives Them." *Marketing News* 51, no. 1, 24–25.

Achen, R.M. 2017. "Measuring Social Media Marketing: Moving towards a Relationship-Marketing Approach." *Managing Sport & Leisure* 22, no. 1, 33–53.

Ahmed, Q.M., A. Qazi, I. Hussain, and S. Ahmed. 2019. "Impact of Social Media Marketing on Brand Loyalty: The Mediating Role of Brand Consciousness." *Journal of Managerial Sciences* 13, no. 2, pp. 201–213.

Ahuja, Y., and I. Loura. "5Ps: A Conceptual Framework for Digital Marketing Campaign." *ASBM Journal of Management* 11, no. 2, pp. 65–77.

American Marketing Association. 2020. "Definitions of Marketing." https://ama.org/the-definition-of-marketing-what-is-marketing/

Appel, G., L. Grewel, R. Hadi, and A.T. Stephen. 2020. "The Future of Social Media in Marketing". *Journal of the Academy of Marketing Science* 48, no. 1, pp. 79–95.

Aswani, R., A.K. Kar, P.V. Ilavarasan, and Y.K. Dwivedi. 2018. "Search Engine Marketing is not all gold: Insights from Twitter and SEOClerks." *International Journal of Information Management* 38, pp. 107–116.

Beig, F.A., and M.F. Khan. 2018. "Impact of Social Media Marketing on Brand Experience: A Study of Select Apparel Brands on Facebook." *Vision* (09722629) 22, no. 3, pp. 264–275.

Blackston, M. 2000. "Observations: Building Brand Equity by Managing the Brand's Relationships." *Journal of Advertising Research* 40, no. 6, pp. 101–105.

Brakus, J.J., B. Schmitt, and L. Zarantonello. 2009. "Brand Experience: What is it? How is it Measured? Does it affect Loyalty?" *Journal of Marketing* 73, no. 3, pp. 52–68.

Chaffey, D., and P.R. Smith. 2017. *Digital Marketing Excellence*. New York, NY: Routledge.

Cluley, R., W. Green, and R. Owen. 2020. "The Changing Role of the Marketing Researcher in the Age of Digital Technology: Practitioner Perspectives on the Digitization of Marketing Research." *International Journal of Market Research* 62, no. 1, pp. 27–42.

Coll, P., and J.L. Mico-Sanz. 2019. "Influencer Marketing in the Growth Hacking Strategy of Digital Brands." *Observatorio (OBS*)* 13, no. 2, pp. 87–105.

Content Marketing Institute. 2020. "B2B Content Marketing 2020; Benchmarks, Budgets, and Trends-North America." https://contentmarketinginstitute. com/wp-content/uploads/2019/10/2020_B2B_Research_Final.pdf

Dick, A.S., and K. Basu. 1994. "Customer Loyalty: Toward an integrated conceptual framework". *Journal of the Academy of Marketing Science*, no. 2, 99. doi:10.1177/0092070394222001

Dodson, I. 2016. *The Art of Digital Marketing: The Definitive Guide to Creating Strategic, Targeted, and Measurable Online Campaigns.* Hoboken, New Jersey: John Wiley & Sons.

Drummond, C., T. O'Toole, and H. McGrath. 2020. "Digital Engagement Strategies and Tactics in Social Media Marketing." *European Journal of Marketing* 54, no. 6, pp. 1247–1280.

Email Tool Tester. 2020. "Email Deliverability: A Detailed look at the Best-Performing Tools". https://emailtooltester.com/en/email-deliverability-test/

Faulds, D., W.G. Mangold, P.S. Raju, and S. Valsalan. 2018. "The Mobile Shopping Revolution: Redefining the consumer decision process." *Business Horizons* 61, no. 2, pp. 323–338.

FTC. 2020. "CAN-SMAP Act: A Compliance Guide for Business." https://ftc. gov/tips-advice/business-center/guidance/can-spam-act-compliance-guide-business

Gosline, R.R., J. Lee, and G. Urban. 2017. "The Power of Consumer Stories in Digital Marketing: New Research Finds that Sharing Consumers' Positive Stories about a Brand can be a Highly Effective Online Marketing Strategy." *MIT Sloan Management Review* 58, no. 4, 10–13. http://ilp.mit.edu/media/ news_articles/smr/2017/58424.pdf

Hickman, E., H. Kharouf, and H. Sekhon. 2020. "An Omnichannel Approach to Retailing: Demystifying and Identifying the Factors Influencing an Omnichannel Experience." *International Review of Retail, Distribution & Consumer Research* 30, no. 3, pp. 266–288.

Hollebeek, L.D., and K. Macky. 2019. "Digital Content Marketing's Role in Fostering Consumer Engagement, Trust, and Value: Framework, Fundamental Propositions, and Implications." *Journal of Interactive Marketing* 45, pp. 27–41.

Hubspot. 2020a. "The Ultimate List of Email Marketing Stats for 2020." https:// blog.hubspot.com/marketing/email-marketing-stats

Hubspot. 2020b. "The ultimate list of Marketing Statistics for 2020." https:// hubspot.com/marketing-statistics

Hudák, M., E. Kianičková, and R. Madleňák. 2017. "The Importance of E-mail Marketing in E-commerce." *Procedia Engineering* 192, pp. 342–347.

Jacobson, J., A. Gruzd, and A. Hernandez-Garcia. 2020. "Social Media Marketing: Who is Watching the Watchers?" *Journal of Retailing and Consumer Services* 53.

Kapferer, J.N. 2004. *The New Strategic Brand Management: Creating and Sustaining Brand Equity Long Term.* London: Kogan Page.

Kannan, P.K., and Hongshuang "Alice" Li. 2017. "Digital marketing: A framework, review and research agenda." *International Journal of Research in Marketing* 34, no. 1, pp. 22–45.

Keller, K. 2013. *Strategic Brand Management,* 4th ed. Upper Saddle River, NJ: Pearson/Prentice Hall.

Kolekar, S., M. Chaudhari, and Y. Patil. 2018. "Current Trends in Personalization and Targeting in Digital Marketing." *International Conference on Ongoing Research in Management & IT,* 298–309.

Kotler, P., H. Kartajaya, and I. Setiawan. 2017. *Marketing 4.0: Moving from Traditional to Digital.* Hoboken, New Jersey: John Wiley & Sons.

Kumar, A., and J. Salo. 2018. "Effects of Link Placements in Email Newsletters on their Click-through Rate." *Journal of Marketing Communications* 24, no. 5, pp. 535–548.

Lemon, K., and P.C. Verhoef. 2016. "Understanding Customer Experience Throughout the Customer Journey." *Journal of Marketing* 80, pp. 69–96.

Litmus. 2018. "Email Client Market Share Trends for the First Half of 2018." https://litmus.com/blog/email-client-market-share-trends-first-half-of-2018/

Mahoney, L.M., and T. Tang. 2017. *Strategic Social Media: From Marketing to Social Change.* n.p.: John Wiley & Sons.

Mark, T., J. Bulla, R. Niraj, I. Bulla, and W. Schwarzwaller. 2019. "Catalogue as a Tool for Reinforcing Habits: Empirical Evidence from a Multichannel Retailer." *International Journal of Research in Marketing* 36, no. 4, pp. 528–541.

Melancon, J.P., and V. Dalakas. 2018. "Consumer Social Voice in the Age of Social Media: Segmentation Profiles and Relationship Marketing Strategies." *Business Horizons* 61, no. 1, pp. 157–167.

Micheaux, A., and B. Bosio. 2019. "Customer Journey Mapping as a New Way to Teach Data-Driven Marketing as a Service." *Journal of Marketing Education* 41, no. 2, pp. 127–140.

Pandley, N., P. Naval, and A.S. Rathore. 2020. "Digital Marketing for B2B Organizations: Structured Literature Review and Future Research Directions." *Journal of Business & Industrial Marketing* 35, no. 7, pp. 1191–1204.

Poulis, A., I. Rizomyliotis, and K. Kinstantiylaki. 2017. *Digital Branding Fever.* New York NY: Business Expert Press.

Rogers, J. 2017. "Social Media Content and Brand Loyalty: A Quantitative Study of the Determinants of Engagement for Gen X Females." *Dissertation Abstracts International Section A: Humanities and Social Sciences.* ProQuest Information & Learning.

Romo, Z.F.G., I. Garcia-Medina and N.P. Romero. 2017. "Storytelling and Social Networking as Tools for Digital and Mobile Marketing of Luxury Fashion Brands." *International Journal of Interactive Mobile Technologies* 11, no. 6, 136–149. doi:10.3991/ijim.v11i6.7511

Statista. 2020a. "Number of smartphone users worldwide from 2016 to 2021." https://statista.com/statistics/330695/number-of-smartphone-users-worldwide/

Statista. 2020b. "Global Spam Volume as Percentage of Total E-Mail Traffic from January 2014 to March 2020, by Month." https://statista.com/statistics/420391/spam-email-traffic-share/

Slijepčević, M., I. Radojevic, and N. Peric. 2020. "Considering Modern Trends in Digital Marketing." *Marketing (0354-3471)* 51, no. 1, 34–42. doi:10.5937/markt2001034s

Turner, P., and S. Turner. 2011. "Is Stereotyping Inevitable When Designing with Personas?" *Design Studies* 32, pp. 34–44.

Tuten, T., and M. Solomon. 2018. *Social Media Marketing.* Thousand Oaks, California: Sage Publications.

Wagner, G., H. Schramm-Klein, and S. Steinmann. 2020. "Online retailing Across E-Channels and E-Channel Touchpoints: Empirical Studies of Consumer Behavior in the Multichannel E-Commerce Environment." *Journal of Business Research* 107, pp. 256–270.

Word of Mouth Marketing Association. 2010. "Influencer Handbook." https://painepublishing.com/wp-content/uploads/2015/06/Influencer-Handbook-v4-2.pdf

About the Author

Dr. Jessica Rogers holds a BS in Business Administration and Marketing, an MS in Marketing, and a PhD in Business Administration with a specialization in Marketing. Her research centers around organic social media marketing engagement, brand loyalty, and Gen X females.

Dr. Rogers is both nationally and locally recognized in the digital marketing education arena. She has been recognized by Hubspot as an innovative professor of digital marketing, BSchools.org 20 Digital and Social Media Marketing Professors to know, as well as Social Media Marketing Magazines "Top Marketing Professors on Twitter." Dr. Rogers contributes to numerous top social and digital marketing blogs, is one of the founding members of Hubspot's Education Partner Program and has received several awards in teaching excellence.

Dr. Rogers has taught both undergraduate and graduate level courses in Marketing for over a decade, and has 16 years of field experience in operations, management, sales, and marketing prior to transitioning into Higher Education. Jessica is a member of the American Marketing Association and Academy of Marketing Science. She also serves as an editorial board member for academic journals.

Index

OTHER TITLES IN THE DIGITAL AND SOCIAL MEDIA MARKETING AND ADVERTISING COLLECTION

Naresh Malhotra, Georgia Tech, Editor

- *Make Your Nonprofit Social* by Lindsay Chambers, Jennifer Morehead and Heather Sallee
- *Marketing in the Digital World* by Avinash Kapoor
- *Digital Marketing Management, Second Edition* by Debra Zahay
- *Make Your Business Social* by Lindsay Chambers, Jennifer Morehead and Heather Sallee
- *Social Media Marketing, Second Edition* by Emi Moriuchi
- *Tell Me About Yourself* by Stavros Papakonstantinidis
- *The Seven Principles of Digital Business Strategy* by Niall McKeown and Mark Durkin
- *Digital Branding Fever* by Athanasios Poulis, Loannis Rizomyliotis and Kleopatra Konstantoulaki
- *Social Media Marketing* by Emi E. Moriuchi
- *R U #SoLoMo Ready?* by Stavros Papakonstantinidis, Athanasios Poulis and Prokopis Theodoridis
- *Fostering Brand Community Through Social Media* by William F. Humphrey, Jr., Debra A. Laverie and Shannon B. Rinaldo
- *Mobile Commerce* by Esther Swilley
- *Digital Privacy in the Marketplace* by George Milne

Concise and Applied Business Books

The Collection listed above is one of 30 business subject collections that Business Expert Press has grown to make BEP a premiere publisher of print and digital books. Our concise and applied books are for...

- Professionals and Practitioners
- Faculty who adopt our books for courses
- Librarians who know that BEP's Digital Libraries are a unique way to offer students ebooks to download, not restricted with any digital rights management
- Executive Training Course Leaders
- Business Seminar Organizers

Business Expert Press books are for anyone who needs to dig deeper on business ideas, goals, and solutions to everyday problems. Whether one print book, one ebook, or buying a digital library of 110 ebooks, we remain the affordable and smart way to be business smart. For more information, please visit www.businessexpertpress.com, or contact sales@businessexpertpress.com.